Catholic Church History
From A to Z

Catholic Church History
From A to Z

An Inspirational Dictionary

Alan Schreck

CHARIS

SERVANT PUBLICATIONS
ANN ARBOR, MICHIGAN

Charis Books is an imprint of Servant Publications especially designed to serve Roman Catholics.

Servant Publications Mission Statement
We are dedicated to publishing books that spread the gospel of Jesus Christ, help Christians to live in accordance with that gospel, promote renewal in the church, and bear witness to Christian unity.

Scripture quotes are taken from the Revised Standard Version of the Bible, copyrighted 1946, 1952, 1971 by the Division of Christian Education of the National Council of Churches of Christ in the USA. Used by permission.

Servant Publications
P.O. Box 8617
Ann Arbor, MI 48107
www.servantpub.com

Cover design: PAZ Design Group, Salem, Oregon

02 03 04 05 10 9 8 7 6 5 4 3 2 1

Printed in the United States of America
ISBN 1-56955-179-0

Introduction

To call a dictionary, of any kind, "inspiring" is to set forth a challenge. Yet the lives of the saints and other holy women and men who have followed Christ faithfully are inspiring. This dictionary offers brief biographical sketches of many of God's servants in the history of the Church, as well as sketches of other significant movements, groups, and events in Catholic history. I hope that these will inspire the reader to study further the history of the Church.

A time line is provided at the beginning of the book so that you may see at a glance some of the most important figures, groups, and events in each century or period of the Church's life. Each item on the time line has an article devoted to it in this dictionary.

An asterisk (*) after a word or phrase indicates a relevant entry in the dictionary under that (or a closely related) heading.

I want to express special thanks to Kasia Ostrowski, who contributed the entry on St. Edmund Campion.

The scope of this book allows me to include only some of the most prominent individuals, movements, and events in the history of the Catholic Church, especially of the Latin rite. This is not to deny the significance of great figures and elements from other streams of Christianity and even various saints that are honored by Eastern rite Catholics or within the many ethnic and cultural heritages that are represented in the Catholic Church. As in the "Liturgy of Hours," saints and figures are included in this dictionary on the basis of their universal ("catholic") recognition. I have also tried to focus on individuals, movements, and groups whose lives and influence have affected significantly the direction and history of the Church in some way, though it must be acknowledged that many of the real "movers and shakers" of God's kingdom on earth are hidden, invisible to history, and known only to God himself.

I apologize in advance for any omissions that may inadvertently occur in the pages that follow. May the lives of these figures continue to instruct, warn, guide, and inspire us!

Alan Schreck, Ph.D.

A

Abelard, Peter (1079–1142)

The brilliant French "bad boy" of early medieval theology and philosophy, Abelard is known best by many for his ill-fated love affair with his student, Heloise. In theology, he raised critical questions in order to understand belief, but has been accused of skepticism as a result. His doctrine of the Trinity was condemned by a Council of Soissons (1121), and other teaching at the Council of Sens (1140). His work *Sic et Non* ("Yes and No") is a collection of seemingly contradictory teachings of the fathers of the Church set side by side. He hoped that the reader would grow through seeking to reconcile them.

One of his chief theological opponents was St. Bernard of Clairvaux,* who attacked Abelard's rationalism. Abelard also was a critic of the philosophical realism of William of Champeaux. In his last years, Abelard lived at Cluny, and through the help of Peter the Venerable was reconciled with St. Bernard and restored to communion with the Catholic Church before his death.

Acton, Lord John (1834–1902)

An influential nineteenth-century English Catholic, Acton was (with German historian Johann Döllinger*) a vocal opponent of the definition of papal infallibility at Vatican I and of Pope Pius IX's* *Syllabus of Errors.* He had taken over John Henry Newman's* editorship of *The Rambler* and changed its name to *Home and Foreign Review* in 1862, until he suspended the paper in 1864 for fear of condemnation through the *Syllabus.* Acton remained a Catholic but focused on his career as an historian at Cambridge. He is known for his dictum "Power tends to corrupt, and absolute power corrupts absolutely."

Adam, Karl (1876–1966)

Adam was an influential twentieth-century German theologian and priest who taught at the University of Tübingen from 1919 to 1949. His writings, including *Christ Our Brother* (1926), *The Christ of Faith* (1954), and *The Spirit of Catholicism* (1924), were widely read. He anticipated the modern Catholic ecumenical movement in his openness to the insights of other Christians, while maintaining Catholic orthodoxy.

Aidan, St. (d. 651)

Aidan was a monk of the famous monastery of Iona in Scotland. In 635 he was consecrated bishop of the Isle of Lindisfarne near the British coast. From there he engaged in many missionary journeys to mainland England, planting the Celtic form of Christianity. He also cared for the poor ransomed slaves and trained young men to become future leaders of the Church and for the nation. (Feast, August 31.)

Alacoque, St. Margaret Mary (1647–90)

Paray-le-Monial in France has become a great center of pilgrimage because of Jesus' revelation of the love of his Sacred Heart to a simple sister of St. Jeanne de Chantal's* Visitation Order: St. Margaret Mary Alacoque. As a child, Margaret Mary was devout and bore much suffering, both physically (she was paralyzed for four years) and emotionally, as her family was often unsympathetic and later insisted that she marry. But in 1671 she fulfilled a vow she had made to enter the Visitation Convent, subse-quently serving as novice mistress and assistant superior.

Beginning in December 1673 she received revelations of Christ, who showed her his heart surrounded by a crown of thorns and promised special graces through receiving Holy Communion on the first Friday of each month, making holy hours of prayer on Thursday, and the establishment of a feast day honoring the Sacred Heart. Jesus, in revealing his Sacred Heart, said, "Behold this heart that has so loved men that it has spared nothing." After eighteen months the revelations ceased, and St. Margaret Mary suffered misunderstanding and rejection in her order.

With the help of her Jesuit confessor, Blessed Claude de la Colombiè, S.J., the opposition softened and the "Apostle of the Sacred Heart" began to be recognized for her holiness. She was canonized by Pope Benedict XV in 1920. (Feast, October 16.)

Albertus Magnus, St. (c. 1200–1280)

"Albert the Great" was regarded as the most learned man of his age and is known as the "Universal Doctor" because of the breadth of his knowledge, especially of the natural sciences, philosophy, and theology. Born in southern Germany, he entered the Dominican order and studied theology in Cologne and then in Paris beginning in 1245. In Paris he began studying Aristotle's philosophy and taught the young Thomas Aquinas.*

Albert returned to Cologne (with Thomas) in 1248 to start a Dominican house of studies, and there wrote or lectured on Peter* Lombard's *Sentences*, Dionysius'* writings, and Aristotle's *Ethics*. Although he served for three years as prior general for the Dominicans in Germany and two years as bishop of Ratisbon, most of his life he spent writing and teaching in Germany, especially Cologne. His influence was important in defending the mendicant orders against their critics.

He defended as well the teachings of his former pupil, St. Thomas Aquinas,* who also used Aristotle as an important source. Albert was credited with making Aristotle "intelligible to the Latins" and for defending the unity of faith and reason. He was canonized in 1931 and declared a Doctor of the Church. (Feast, November 15.)

Albigensians

The Albigensians (named for the village of Albi, a center of the group in southern France) believed in the existence of a good god and an evil god—good being pure spirit, and evil manifesting itself in anything material. This theological dualism goes back to the ancient Persian teacher Mani (c. 215–76; his followers are called Manichaeans), but in the Middle Ages they took the name "Cathari" (the pure) or Cathars. This austere group opposed both the material wealth of the Catholic Church and its sacraments, which involved material things.

The Church sought to convert the Albigensians, but when a papal legate, Peter of Castebran, was murdered in 1209, the pope launched a military campaign or crusade against them, led by Simon de Montfort. Montfort won a key battle at Muret in 1213, and thereafter the Inquisition* (established by Pope Gregory IX*) completed the work of rooting out the heresy by the end of the thirteenth century.

Alcuin (c. 735–804)

Alcuin achieved renown as Charlemagne's* household tutor and "minister of education" for his far-flung empire. Born in England, Alcuin was educated at the cathedral school at York and remained there forty years, becoming headmaster around 766. When his archbishop sent deacon Alcuin on a mission to Rome, he met Charlemagne, who offered him a post at the royal court. Later in his life (796) he was named abbot of St. Martin's monastery at Tours.

Alcuin's main achievement was to promote proper Latin usage (which was woefully abused and corrupted) and to encourage education. He also directed the standardization of the liturgy in Charlemagne's empire. Though not an original scholar, he did produce a few literary works, such as *On the Bishops, Kings, and Saints of York*. Tragically, the library he had amassed at York was totally destroyed by Viking invasions, and the heritage of English scholarship only survived because Alcuin had brought it to the Continent. He is honored as an important preserver of Western culture.

Alexander of Hales (c. 1186–1245)

A British scholar who studied and taught theology at the University of Paris, Alexander became a Franciscan in 1236, the first holder of a permanent Franciscan chair at Paris. He set a precedent by choosing the *Sentences* of Peter Lombard* as his primary classroom text. Besides his glosses on the *Sentences*, he wrote *Quaestiones* in theology and began a *Summa Theologica* that was completed by other Franciscans. A founder of the Franciscan school of theology at the University of Paris, he is known as the "Doctor Irrefragibilis" (the "Irrefutable Doctor").

Ambrose, St. (c. 339–97)

As bishop of Milan from 373–97, Ambrose was the most influential spiritual leader of his time. He is recognized as one of the four "fathers of the Latin Church," along with St. Augustine,* St. Jerome,* and Pope St. Gregory the Great.* Born in Trier, Gaul, he was raised in a Catholic family and received a classical education that included Greek, preparing him to become a lawyer.

He was not baptized as a youth, but studied the faith under the priest Simplicianus. About 370, he was a provincial governor residing in Milan. When he went to oversee the election of a new bishop, the people acclaimed Ambrose bishop, though he was only a catechumen (studying to be baptized).

As bishop, he was influential in protecting the Church against civil authorities and seeing that the Christian rulers were obeying the moral law. His most famous intervention took place when he commanded the Eastern emperor Theodosius* to do public penance in Milan for ordering a massacre of Christians in Thessalonica. (Later he preached Theodosius' funeral sermon and praised him for seeking to unite the East and West in one faith.)

Ambrose's preaching was also instrumental in the conversion of St. Augustine,* who was baptized by the bishop in 387. Not only a true pastor of souls and an influential preacher, St. Ambrose—through his ministry as bishop—revealed the power of the Church's influence in Roman politics and society in the later fourth century. (Feast, December 7.)

Anabaptists

"Anabaptist" literally means "rebaptizer." It was a label given to a variety of groups in the Protestant Reformation that rejected infant baptism and generally interpreted the Bible's view of the Church and its life more radically than the Lutherans. The title "Anabaptist" became a derisive term, and groups so labeled were often persecuted by both Catholics and Protestants.

The first group of Anabaptists emerged in Zurich, Switzerland, in 1525, in opposition to belief in infant baptism. These Christians believed that only adult baptism was valid. Of the other bodies later called Anabaptists, some advocated armed revolution to achieve their ends (such as the group led by Thomas Müntzer), while others, such as Menno Simons (founder of the Mennonites) and the Swiss Brethren (represented by Balthasar Hubmaier) were pacifists. Müntzer, Simons, and Hubmaier were all Catholic priests before departing on these diverse Anabaptist paths.

Anselm of Canterbury, St. (c. 1033–1109)

Regarded as the most important Christian thinker between St. Augustine* and St. Thomas Aquinas,* Anselm was declared a Doctor of the Church by Pope Clement XI in 1720. His *Monologion* and *Proslogion*

(1078–79) present an ontological argument for God's existence: God is "that than which nothing greater can be thought."

In *Cur Deus Homo* (1095), Anselm presents Christ's incarnation and death as a necessary "satisfaction" to atone for human sin. Anselm insists on the necessity of both faith and reason to grasp the mystery of God, with faith as the starting point: "I believe in order that I may understand" (*"credo ut intelligam"*).

Anselm was born in Italy and entered monastic life at Bec in France, studying under his countryman, Lanfranc. Anselm succeeded Lanfranc both as prior at Bec and later as archbishop of Canterbury. As archbishop Anselm had a stormy career, boldly asserting the rights of the Church over the attempts of the English king William II to control it through lay investiture. Anselm was never formally canonized, but his feast is celebrated on the day of his death (April 21).

Ansgar, St. (801–65)

"The Apostle of the North," Ansgar was a Benedictine monk from the Picardy region of France who volunteered to spread the Christian faith in Denmark after the conversion of its King Harald in 826. He was named bishop of Hamburg (832) and archbishop of Bremen (848), but his first love was evangelization. He built the first Christian church in Sweden and then returned to Denmark, where he converted Erik, king of Jutland. By the time of his death in 865, Ansgar had converted much of Denmark and many Swedes, though after his death both countries relapsed into almost complete paganism until gradual reconversion began in 965. (Feast, February 3.)

Anthony of Padua St. (1191–1231)

Around 1217 a bright young man named Ferdinand from Lisbon, Portugal, joined the Canons Regular of St. Augustine at Coimbra. However, he soon was attracted by the evangelical lifestyle of a new order that moved into the region, the "Friars Minor," followers of St. Francis of Assisi.* The story of the first Franciscan martyrs in Morocco led him to join their order in 1220, taking the name Anthony.

He soon set off to Morocco to preach the gospel and seek a martyr's death. God had other plans. Upon landing in North Africa Anthony became gravely ill. Instead of returning to Portugal, his boat was blown off course to Sicily, where he recovered and accompanied a group of Franciscan friars to the famous General Chapter of 1221 in Assisi.

For reasons now unknown, Anthony stayed in Italy after the chapter until his extraordinary gift for preaching was discovered when he was asked to given an impromptu ordination sermon at Forli. He was named the preacher of the province of Romagna, Italy. Anthony's reputation for theological knowledge and preaching grew, until Francis himself (in 1222 or 23) directed Anthony to teach the friars theology, as long as it did not detract from their prayer and devotion.

In 1224 Anthony went to France to attend a chapter, where he preached powerful sermons against the Cathar heresy. After Francis' death in 1226, Anthony returned to Italy and was made minister provincial of Romagna. Padua was a chief city in the province.

Toward the end of his life, Anthony was relieved of his office and spent more time in Padua, completing his *Sunday Sermons*. He preached before the Roman Curia in 1230, and Pope Gregory IX called him the "Ark of the New Covenant" because of his wisdom. Anthony returned to Padua and worked on sermons for saints' feast days until his death in 1231.

In 1946 he was declared a Doctor of the Church by Pope Pius XII.* He is known as the "Evangelic Doctor" and is has long been invoked by the faithful for help in finding lost articles. Anthony is often portrayed holding the Christ Child. (Feast, June 13.)

Antony of Egypt, St. (c. 251–356)
The title "father of monasticism" could be applied to a number of Christians who followed the path of radical, ascetic imitation of Jesus Christ in the late third century. Antony deserves this title because of his sanctity, his widespread personal influence, and the renown he gained through the *Life of Antony*—written by his friend, St. Athanasius,* patriarch of Alexandria.

Antony was born in Coma, Egypt, of affluent Christian parents, whose death left Antony with a large estate when he was only a youth. But the spiritual heritage they gave to

Antony was even greater. At church one day he was moved by the words of the Gospel: "If you would be perfect, go, sell what you possess and give to the poor, and you will have treasure in heaven" (Mt 19:21). He responded literally to this call, placed his younger sister in the care of some holy women, and began to live a life of self-denial or asceticism.

Athanasius writes of him: "He worked with his hands ... he prayed constantly ... he paid such close attention to what was read that nothing from Scripture did he fail to take in ... and in him the memory took the place of books. Leading his life in this way, Antony was loved by all."

Soon Antony heard the Lord call him to greater solitude, so he lived in an abandoned fortress for twenty years, where he constantly engaged in prayer and spiritual battle with demons. He is thus also known as the father of the "eremetical" life—the life of a hermit. After twenty years he emerged from solitude, not withdrawn and emaciated, but full of the radiance of Christ. He forcefully "persuaded many to take up the solitary life," Athanasius reports. "And so, from then on, there were monasteries in the mountains and the desert was made a city by monks, who left their own people and registered themselves for the citizenship in the heavens."

Although some scholars question the accuracy of Athanasius' account, it is confirmed by Antony's own letters that he supported St. Pachomius* in the founding of monastic communities (*coenobia*) in Egypt and assisted St. Athanasius in refuting the Arian heresy. When Antony died at the age of 105, the ascetic or monastic movement that he pioneered was flourishing throughout the eastern Roman Empire and had even begun to take root in the West. (Feast, January 17.)

Apollinarianism

This heresy was named after Apollinarius (or Appolinaris), bishop of Laodicea in fourth-century Syria. He so emphasized the divinity of Jesus that he said that the *Logos* or Word of God replaced Christ's rational human soul. Thus, the full humanity of Jesus Christ was denied, as was pointed out by St. Gregory of Nazianzus* and others who opposed Apollinarius' view. This teaching was condemned as a heresy by Pope Damasus* (pope 366–384) and by

the First Council of Constantinople*
in 381.

Apostles

The ministry of spreading the good news of Jesus Christ and founding local churches is the special gift (*charism*) of the apostle (see 1 Cor 12:28, Eph 4:11). "Apostle" literally means "one who is sent." From among his disciples, Jesus selected, trained, and sent out twelve to be his special representatives. These twelve apostles are Simon Peter, Andrew, James and John (the sons of Zebedee), Philip, Bartholomew (or Nathaniel), Thomas, Matthew, James the son of Alphaeus, Thaddaeus (or Jude, son of James), Simon (the Zealot), and Judas Iscariot (see Mt 10:2-4; Mk 3:16-19; Lk 6:14-16; Jn 1:35-51).

St. Paul also called himself an apostle because the risen Jesus appeared to him (see 1 Cor 4:9; 15:7-10). Paul soon became known as the "Apostle to the Gentiles" for his ministry among those not of Jewish origin.

The apostles and their fellow workers (such as Barnabas, Timothy, Silas, John Mark, and others) are the "foundation" upon which Jesus built his Church (see Eph 2:20). Hence the Church has sought to faithfully preserve and pass on their teaching—the "apostolic teaching" or "apostolic tradition"—and their office of leadership, the "apostolic succession" of bishops, who continued the ministry of the apostles.

Many traditions have survived about the work and fate of Jesus' apostles, though not all of these can be verified historically from secular sources. Peter and Paul are said to have died in Rome in Nero's persecution in 64. (Feasts: SS. Peter and Paul, June 29; Dedication of their basilicas in Rome, November 18; Chair of Peter, February 22; Conversion of St. Paul, January 25.)

St. Thomas is said to have preached among the Parthians and planted the Church in India. ("St. Thomas Christians" exist in India to this day.) He is believed to have been martyred near Madras, India. (Feast, July 3.)

SS. Simon and Jude (feast, October 28) are associated because an apocryphal work about their lives claims that they were missionaries together in Persia and were martyred there. St. Jude, called Thaddaeus in Matthew 10:3 and Mark 3:18, is widely venerated as the "patron saint of hopeless cases."

Apostles' Creed

This creed, developed from the Old Roman Creed, first emerged in its present form in the early eighth century. It became the standard creed used for baptism in the Western Catholic Church in the early Middle Ages, and through Charlemagne's* influence it was used and accepted throughout his vast dominion in Europe.

Apostolic Fathers

This title has been given to prominent Christian leaders who wrote in the era immediately following the time of the apostles,* and who were directly or indirectly associated with them. Some of the writings of the apostolic fathers, such as the *Shepherd of Hermas* and the *Epistle of Barnabas*, were considered for inclusion in the canon of the New Testament. The writings of the apostolic fathers are characterized by a simple direct style and a nonphilosophical presentation of Christian faith and ideals.

The authority of these fathers is based on the tradition and teaching handed on to them by the apostles* and the leaders (especially the bishops) who immediately succeeded the apostles. Though not considered to be divinely "inspired," their writings are often inspirational and teach us much about the life, doctrine, practices, and circumstances of the Church in the late first century and early second century. The Catholic understanding of Church hierarchy, the sacraments, liturgy, devotions, and moral teaching are reflected in their initial form in these writings.

The apostolic fathers include Pope St. Clement of Rome,* St. Ignatius of Antioch,* Hermas,* and St. Polycarp of Smyrna.* The early Christian authors Papias and Quadratus are sometimes also listed among them. Other writings of the apostolic fathers, whose authors are unknown or uncertain, include the *Epistle to Diognetus*, the *Martyrdom of Polycarp*, the *Epistle of Barnabas*, the *Didache** (or *Teaching of the Twelve Apostles*), and the *Second Letter of Clement of Rome*, which is most probably an early Christian homily.

Aquinas, St. Thomas (c. 1225–74)

Known as one of the greatest intellects in the Church's history, Thomas is called the "Angelic Doctor" or the "Common Doctor" and is the patron saint of Catholic schools, colleges, and universities. A son of Count Landuff of Aquino, Thomas was born in Roccasecca, Italy, around 1224 and began his studies at age five at the famous Benedictine monastery of Monte Cassino. His parents' plan was for Thomas to become a Benedictine, but when he went to study for a year at the University of Naples, he encountered the young Dominican order and decided to join them.

The young man's parents, however, held him prisoner in hopes that he would change his mind. But eventually they relented, and in 1245 Thomas began his studies in Rome and Paris as a Dominican, where he was jokingly called "The Dumb Ox" by his classmates. His teacher, St. Albertus Magnus,* saw his genius, and later took Thomas to Cologne, where he was ordained in 1248.

Returning to Paris, Aquinas lectured on Scripture and on the *Sentences* of Peter Lombard*, but he was also forced to defend the new mendicant orders from the attacks of their critics. He and St. Bonaventure* received their doctorates in theology in 1257, and Thomas began to write the *Summa Contra Gentiles* for Dominican missionaries. He was called back to Italy, where he produced a number of works (such

as a liturgy for the Feast of Corpus Christi) for Pope Urban IV.

In 1265, he began his greatest work, the *Summa Theologiae,* in Rome. However, his most prolific period of scholarship was in Paris between 1268 and 1272. There he defended the proper use of Aristotelian philosophy against the extreme Aristotelians — especially Siger of Brabant and the followers of the Muslim philosopher Averroes—and wrote against the anti-Aristotelians John Peckham and Stephen Tempier, bishop of Paris. He lectured on Scripture and theological themes and continued to write the *Summa Theologiae.*

In the spring of 1272, St. Thomas returned to Italy, where he established a program of studies in Naples, preached during Lent, and continued work on his *Summa Theologiae.* On December 6, 1273, St. Thomas had a mystical experience, which led him to say: "Everything I have written seems like straw compared to what I have seen and what has been revealed to me." After that, St. Thomas taught and wrote no more. He died only three months later while traveling to the Second Council of Lyons.*

It is practically impossible here to exaggerate Thomas' contribution to Catholic theology. His theology and philosophy were new and controversial in his day, but after his death he was canonized (1323) and declared a Doctor of the Church in the tumultuous sixteenth century (1567). "Thomism" became a major branch of medieval scholasticism—the theology of the schools or universities.

In the nineteenth and twentieth centuries there was a rebirth of interest in Thomas' teaching, resulting in a "Neo-Thomism" and a "transcendental Thomism," among other forms. In 1879, Pope Leo XIII* required the study of Thomas in seminaries, and tribute has been paid to his work by Pope Pius XI,* Pope Paul VI,* and the Second Vatican* Council. (Feast, January 28.)

Arius (c. 250–c. 336)

Ordained a priest in Alexandria early in the fourth century, Arius was the author of one of the most pernicious heresies ever to afflict the Church. He taught that although Jesus is Lord and Savior, he is not equal to God the Father, but is instead the highest creature of God. After all, Arius argued, Jesus said, "The Father is greater than I" (Jn 14:28).

The heresy spread and was so divisive that finally the emperor Constantine* called all the Eastern bishops to a Council at Nicea* in 325 to determine the truth. This council condemned Arius' teaching, but influential patrons led by Bishop Eusebius of Nicomedia convinced the emperor and many bishops that that Council's decision was mistaken and Arius was correct. Constantine himself ordered the greatest opponent of Arius, St. Athanasius of Alexandria,* to accept Arius back into communion, and exiled Athanasius when he refused.

Although Arius died in Constantinople in 336, his heresy continued to spread until it was condemned once again by the First Council of Constantinople* in 381. By that time, however, some Eastern European tribes had been converted to Arian Christianity, and so the beliefs of Arius continued to plague the Church in later centuries.

Ascetic Movement

As the "age of persecution" of Christians came to a close in the reign of the emperor Constantine* (312–337), a movement emerged of

Christians who renounced worldly ways and embraced a life of intense prayer and self-denial (asceticism) for the sake of Christ. The cradle of this movement was Egypt, where even before Constantine, St. Antony* and others had heard God's call to sell their worldly goods and seek God in prayer and fasting in the deserts of Egypt. (Hence they are often called "the desert fathers.")

This movement is also the beginning of religious communities, as the ascetics voluntarily chose to be celibate, poor, and obedient to Christ and to each other. Communities, even cities, of ascetics sprang up in the deserts of Egypt, with leaders such as St. Pachomius* developing "rules" to order them.

Even though they all came to be called "monks" (from the Greek word *monos,* meaning "alone" or "solitary"), some were truly hermits, living alone (eremitical monasticism, the monasticism of hermits), while others lived in groups or communities called *coenobia* (coenobitical monasticism) or later, "monasteries." The monks were recognized as the new models of radical Christian life after martyrdom had ceased, and pilgrims flocked to the desert to witness their lives and to hear their words or "sayings," which were profound but often puzzling or humorous.

The ascetic or monastic movements had a tremendous impact on Christians beginning in the fourth century. Henceforth, some of the Church's greatest bishops and theologians were ascetics. St. Basil of Caesarea* in the East and, a century later, St. Benedict* in the West wrote "rules" to guide monastic life.

Athanasius, St. (c. 298–373)

Athanasius, patriarch (archbishop) of Alexandria, was one of the great pillars of the ancient Church: patron of the monks, theologian of the full divinity of Jesus Christ and the Holy Spirit, and indomitable defender of the teaching of the Council of Nicea* (325) against the Arian* heresy. Exiled by pro-Arian emperors five times for his stand affirming the truth of Christ's full divinity, the saying was coined "*Athanasius contra mundum,*" which means, "Athanasius against the world."

Though born an Egyptian in Alexandria, Athanasius' education was thoroughly Greek. He was a precocious scholar, penning his brilliant treatise *On the Incarnation of the*

Word at age twenty. His faith had been forged in fire as he grew up through the Diocletian* persecution. He had known martyrs, as well as ascetics who fled to the desert to seek God and escape persecution, including his friend, St. Antony of Egypt,* the "father" of monasticism.

After the emergence of the heresy of Arius, Athanasius attended the Council of Nicea as a deacon. When his bishop, Alexander, died in 328, Athanasius was named patriarch of Alexandria and remained so until his death. While other bishops and emperors waffled, Athanasius remained steadfastly loyal to the teaching of Nicea against Arianism. His periods of exile at their hands did not deter Athanasius, but only led him to strengthen the faith of those he visited in exile, which included the pope in Rome and his beloved monks in the Egyptian desert. He introduced monasticism to the West, especially through his biography of St. Antony.*

In 362 Athanasius called a council in Alexandria, where he convinced the semi-Arian bishops to support the doctrinal formula of Nicea: that the Son is *homoousios* ("one in being with" or "of the same substance as")

the Father. He gained the support of St. Basil the Great* and the other Cappadocian fathers, which led to the final defeat of Arianism* at the First Council of Constantinople* in 381. Athanasius did not live to see that event, but the last seven years of his life were spent in Alexandria, in relative peace, with support for the cause of Nicea* growing ever stronger.

Athanasius promoted the Eastern theology of *theosis* ("deification"), which speaks of the Incarnation giving us a share in the divine nature: "He [Christ] became what we are that he might make us what he is." He also defended the divinity of the Holy Spirit against the Macedonian heresy (*pneumatomachi*), stressing the importance of the Holy Spirit in transforming us into God's image. (Feast, May 2.)

Augustine of Canterbury, St. (d. 604 or 605)

Around the year 595, Augustine, head of a monastery in Rome, was sent along with forty of his monks by Pope St. Gregory I* to evangelize the Anglo-Saxons in England. Although some of the monks were fearful and desired to turn back,

Augustine led them to England, where they succeeded in converting King Ethelbert of Kent and many of his subjects. Augustine established his administration at Canterbury and had a cathedral and a monastery built there.

Twice he met with Celtic bishops from Wales to seek common practices, such as the date of the celebration of Easter, but these efforts were unsuccessful. Not until the Synod of Whitby* (663–64) was this Paschal controversy resolved. Augustine exemplifies the courage of the monk-missionaries of this era, who were loyal to the pope and fervent in their desire to lead all people to Jesus Christ. (Feast, May 27.)

Augustine of Hippo, St. (354–430)

Augustine is widely recognized as the greatest of the Latin fathers of the early Church and one of the most prominent thinkers in the history of Christianity. He was born in Thagaste, North Africa, of a devout Catholic mother, Monica*, and a pagan father, Patricius.

In his autobiography, *The Confessions*, Augustine tells of his youth as a time of both inflamed passions and an insatiable thirst for truth. He dealt with the former by taking a concubine (who later bore him a son, Adeodatus), and the latter by studying the Latin classics of literature and philosophy. He became a teacher of rhetoric, but his mind was absorbed by his quest for true meaning. In spite of his mother's influence, Augustine joined the Manichees, who taught that the body and all matter are inferior to "spirit" and intrinsically evil.

Augustine's blossoming career led him to Rome, but there he became disenchanted with the Manichees and his mercenary students. He moved to Milan, where he taught rhetoric, and listened to the sermons of the Catholic bishop St. Ambrose,* out of professional interest. To Augustine's surprise, Ambrose answered his objections to Christianity, and after a now-famous conversion (see *The Confessions*, 8:12), Augustine was baptized by Ambrose in 387.

Augustine's plan was to spend the rest of his life philosophizing with a small community of friends, but God had other plans for him. After the death of his mother, he returned to North Africa and was seized by the

Catholics in Hippo, a coastal town, and ordained a priest in 392.

For the rest of his life Augustine was absorbed with pastoral duties and teaching the faith. He succeeded Valerius as bishop of Hippo in 396. He confronted the Donatists,* whose schismatic church in North Africa had come to rival the Catholic Church there in size and influence.

The other great theological conflict of the bishop's career was against the heretical monk Pelagius,* who denied the corrupting influence of original sin and overestimated human freedom. With St. Jerome,* Augustine refuted Pelagius and earned the title "Doctor of Grace." As bishop, Augustine wrote hundreds of letters, landmark theological treatises on such topics as the Holy Trinity and grace, and even a "theology of history," *The City of God*, in which St. Augustine refutes the pagan claim that Christianity caused the downfall of the Roman Empire.

He finished this work even as he saw the great Roman Empire being dismantled by invasions. Augustine himself died while the Vandals were besieging Hippo, with the Catholic Church in North Africa doomed to destruction. Yet Augustine will always be known as one who focused on the interior search of each person for God, as the one who prayed to God: "You have made us for yourself, and our hearts are restless until they rest in you" (*Confessions,* 1:1). (Feast, August 28.)

Avignon Papacy
This is the designation for a period from 1309 until 1377 in which the popes resided and governed the Catholic Church from the city of Avignon in southern France. Pope Clement V* was the first pope to reside there, and Pope Gregory XI* was the last, leaving in 1377 in response to the exhortation of St. Catherine of Siena* and others. Because the papacy was dominated by French interests during these years and was exiled from Rome by political influence, this period has also been called the "Babylonian Captivity of the Church."

Bacon, Roger (c. 1214–c. 1292)

Born in England, Bacon studied philosophy at Oxford and taught it at Paris, but in 1247 he turned his attention to natural science and mathematics. He joined the Franciscan order around 1251 and continued his scientific studies. He was suspected of erroneous ideas but won the ear of a French cardinal who became Pope Clement IV.

Bacon wrote his *Opus Maius* (or *Great Work*) explaining his proposed program for the revitalization of Western education (focusing on the study of math, languages, and science), but Pope Clement died before he could make use of it. Later some of Bacon's works were condemned by his Franciscan superiors, and he was imprisoned for a time in 1277. It is said that he produced many inventions (gunpowder, a telescope, eyeglasses), but these claims have been disputed. Bacon is viewed as a pioneer in the exploration of science and mathematics and is sometimes called the *"Doctor Mirabilis"* (the "Amazing Doctor").

Barnabas, Epistle of

Though attributed to St. Barnabas, the companion of St. Paul, this letter was written by an unknown author, probably in Alexandria between 70 and 100. It interprets the Old Testament allegorically, that is, as having symbolic meaning that is fulfilled in Jesus and the New Testament. Also notable is its vivid description of the "two ways": the "way of light" (moral living that leads to salvation) and the "way of darkness." The section of the text about the "two ways" is so similar to part of the *Didache** (or *The Teaching of the Twelve Apostles*) that it is likely that one book borrowed it from another, or that they had a common source.

Basil "the Great," St. (c. 330–79)

In an era of prominent saints, why is St. Basil distinguished as "the Great"? His origins were auspicious; his grandmother Macrina (the elder) was a saint, and among his eight surviving siblings, two were declared saints—Gregory of Nyssa* and Macrina*—and one (Peter) became a bishop. His brother, Gregory, his friend Gregory of Nazianzus,* and he are known today as the "Cappadocian fathers."

Basil studied as a youth in Caesarea,

Constantinople, and finally in Athens, where he met his lifelong friend, Gregory of Nazianzus. He returned to Caesarea to teach, but with the urgings and prayers of the bishop, Basil's lifelong friend Dianus, and his holy sister Macrina, Basil turned his life fully to the Lord. After visiting monasteries in Syria and Egypt, he returned home to live as a hermit in 358.

Here his reputation began to grow. He and his friend St. Gregory founded a monastery in Pontus that was governed by rules developed by Basil between 358 and 364 (called the *Long Rule* and the *Short Rule*). The teaching on the virtue of obedience, on the balance between prayer and work, and other practical aspects of his *Rules* provided a standard for Eastern monasticism.

A second aspect of Basil's greatness was his service to the Church as defender of Nicene* orthodoxy against the Arian* emperors (especially Valens). He left his solitude to serve as a priest in 363 and then as bishop of Caesarea from 370 to his death in 379. His stand against Valens has been compared with St. Ambrose's* courageous action against the emperor Theodosius.* Two years after his death, Arianism was defeated at the First Council of Constantinople* in 381.

St. Basil followed St. Athanasius* in developing the Church's theology of the Holy Spirit, refuting the *Pneumatomachi,* who denied the Holy Spirit's divinity. With St. Gregory of Nazianzus he compiled the *Philocalia,* a selection of writings of Origen* and other Eastern fathers. (Feast, with St. Gregory of Nazianzus, January 2.)

Becket, St. Thomas (c. 1118–70)

At age thirty-six, Thomas (à) Becket was named archdeacon of Canterbury. He made a good impression on King Henry II, who named him chancellor of England a year later, in 1155. Thomas became a close friend of the king, so when the archbishop of Canterbury died, the king appointed Thomas to this post, thinking this would secure state control of the Church.

Thomas, seeing the conflict of interest, was reluctant to become archbisop but yielded to the king's wish. However, after his consecration in 1162, Thomas chose to serve God and the Church first. He decided that he could not abide by the government's "Constitutions of Clarendon" issued in 1164, which limited the Church's freedom, and he opposed the king on a number of issues.

Under pressure from the king, Thomas fled to France and sought the support of Pope Alexander III. After six years of exile, a reconciliation was arranged, and Thomas returned to England amidst cheering throngs. However, within a month he again incurred the king's wrath by suspending bishops who had assisted in the coronation of the king's son at York instead of Canterbury.

Then, in a scene that has been retold and dramatized many times, a group of the king's soldiers (perhaps at his behest) went to Canterbury and murdered Thomas in his cathedral church on the night of December 29, 1170. The world was shocked. Thomas was canonized as a martyr by Pope Alexander III in 1173, and King Henry did public penance at his tomb in Canterbury in 1174.

This tomb became one of the major pilgrimage sites in Europe until Henry VIII* destroyed the shrine in 1538. The shrine is gone, but the memory of the steadfastness of St. Thomas Becket has inspired generations of Christians. (Feast, December 29.)

Bede, St. (c. 673–735)

Known as "Bede the Venerable" and "the Father of English History," Bede is a great scholar-saint of the early Middle Ages. He spent nearly all his adult life writing and teaching at the monastery of Jarrow in England. Besides his famous *History of the English Church and People* (by which we know much about the planting and growth of the Church there), he also wrote two lives of St. Cuthbert (in verse and prose) and many commentaries on sacred Scripture that drew heavily from the writings of SS. Augustine,* Jerome,* Ambrose,* and Gregory the Great* (the four great Latin fathers of the early Church). He also wrote scientific and pedagogical manuals; the most widely used one was on the computation of the date of Easter from the lunar cycle. He was declared a Doctor of the Church by Pope Leo XIII* in 1899. (Feast, May 25.)

Bellarmine, St. Robert (1542–1621)

This Italian theologian was one of the foremost apologists of the Catholic reformation, known especially for the moderation and rationality of his writings in an era fraught with bitter polemics. He was ordained a Jesuit priest in 1570 and taught theology at Louvain until he was appointed to teach at the newly founded Jesuit "Roman College" (later the Gregorian University) in 1576. He devoted himself to scholarship, writing a three-volume defense of the Catholic faith and a treatise on the temporal authority of the pope (in which he denies direct papal authority in temporal matters), as well as assisting in the revision of the Vulgate Bible. He is known for his classic definition of the Church, stressing its visible marks of the profession of faith (creed*), the true sacraments, and the rule of the legitimate pastors (bishops) united with the successor of Peter, the pope.

Bellarmine was made a cardinal in 1599 by Pope Clement VIII and archbishop of Capua in 1602. Despite his prominence, he also served the poor and died nearly penniless. He was canonized in 1930 and declared a Doctor of the Church in 1931 by Pope Pius XI.* (Feast, September 17.)

Benedict, St. (c. 480–c. 550)

Born in the small Italian village of Nursia, Benedict was sent to Rome for a classical education. However, he disdained Rome's worldliness and sought solitude in a cave at Subiaco east of the city. His holy life attracted followers, so he started a community of ascetics.

Later he preached conversion at Monte Cassino (between Rome and Naples), founded his great monastery there, and composed his *Rule* for the community. This *Rule*, which was to become the guide for Western medieval monasticism, stressed a balanced ascetic life of self-discipline, prayer, and work (*ora et labora*), combining spiritual insight and practical wisdom for common life. Silence, obedience, and humility are shown as the three central monastic virtues.

Benedict himself was not well known in his lifetime, nor was he always popular. It is said that some of his own monks tried to kill him by putting poison in his drinking glass, but the glass shattered as he said a blessing over it. The rich heritage of his example, his *Rule*, and the "Benedictine" communities that followed his way of life have earned him the Church's recognition as one of the patron saints of Europe and the "Father of Western Monasticism." (Feast, July 11.)

Bernard of Clairvaux, St. (1090–1153)

Born of noble French parents, Bernard was blessed with zeal, wisdom, and personal magnetism. When he joined the monastery at Cîteaux in 1112 (at age twenty-two), he brought thirty young men with him, including his brothers. Three years later the prior, St. Stephen Harding, sent Bernard to found a new monastery, which was named Clairvaux ("Valley of Light").

Bernard and his monastery quickly became a light for the whole Church. Clairvaux's reputation spread, and Bernard was called upon to serve the Church internationally in numerous capacities: to draw up rules for the order of the Knights Templar, to settle disputes (even in the papal election of 1130), and to preach the ill-fated Second Crusade.* He strongly opposed the new rationalistic theology of Peter Abelard* and Gilbert de la Porré.

Bernard's own writings are the apex in beauty and power of traditional monastic theology; some call him "the last of the Fathers." Among his more than three hundred letters and treatises, the most famous are his treatise on the papacy (*De Consideratione*, sent to Cisterian pope Eugenius III), his treatises on ascetic* spirituality, and his allegorical sermons *On the Song of Songs*. Bernard also had a great devotion to Mary. Known as the *"Doctor Mellifluus"* ("Honey-Sweet Doctor"), he was canonized in 1174 and named a Doctor of the Church in 1830. (Feast, August 20.)

Bernardine of Siena, St. (1380–1444)

Born in Italy, Bernardine was zealous for God from his youth and known especially for his purity. He joined the strict Franciscan "Observants" in 1402. He became one of the most renowned preachers of the age and was especially known as the "Apostle of the Holy Name of Jesus." Declining all offers to become a bishop, this "second St. Paul" (Pope Pius II's name for Bernardine) remained a humble member of his religious community until his death. (Feast, May 20.)

Bernini, Giovanni Lorenzo (1598–1680)

This Italian baroque sculptor and architect first sculpted for the Borghese family (producing *Apollo and Daphne* and *David* in 1623–24), and then was enlisted by Pope Urban VIII to produce architecture and sculpture for St. Peter's Church and the Vatican. Among his most prominent works there are his baldacchino over the main altar in St. Peter's (1624–33), his sculpture of the *Chair of St. Peter* (1657–66) and of *St. Longinus* (1629–35), and the vast colonnade enclosing the piazza in front of St. Peter's (1656–67).

Bérulle, Cardinal Pierre de (1575–1629)

A reformer of the Church in France in the seventeenth century, Bérulle was ordained a priest in 1599. He brought the Discalced Carmelite nuns to Paris (from Spain) in 1604, and in 1611 founded an oratory modeled on St. Philip Neri's* Roman oratory, except Bérulle's became a congregation of priests (known as "Oratorians"). He was influential both in religious and political affairs and was made a cardinal in 1627.

Bérulle's profoundly Christ-centered spirituality led Pope Urban VIII to call him "the Apostle of the Incarnate Word." He advocated a spirituality of total submission to Jesus and Mary, and devotion to the Child Jesus.

Biel, Gabriel (1420–95)

Biel was one of the last prominent medieval scholastic thinkers. He wrote a commentary on Peter* Lombard's *Sentences* but is best known for espousing and developing the nominalist philosophy of William of Ockham.*

Educated in Germany, Biel joined the Brethren of the Common Life* in 1468 and was prior at their houses in Butzbäch (1470) and Urach (1479). With Count Eberhard of Württemberg, he helped found the University of Tübingen and taught theology there. Besides teaching theology, he developed economic theories that were not dependent on theological principles, which reflected the new directions of Renaissance thought. His nominalism is said to have influenced Martin Luther.*

Blondel, Maurice (1861–1949)

A French Catholic philosopher, Blondel taught a philosophy of human acts (*L'Action*, 1893), which opened the way to new philosophical approaches in the tradition of Plato and St. Augustine* (in contrast to the prevalent Aristotelianism/Thomism of his day). Blondel also influenced leading "modernist" thinkers such as Friedrich Hügel, though he was not himself a modernist, remaining a devout Catholic until his death in 1949.

Boethius (c. 480–c. 524)

This brilliant philosopher was pressed into the service of the state by the emperor Theodoric in 510, but was unjustly condemned and executed for treason sometime between 524 and 526. His most famous work, *The Consolation of Philosophy*, recounts the visit of "Lady Philosophy" to Boethius in prison and asserts the ultimate triumph of God's truth and justice in eternity. Although it has been debated whether Boethius was a Christian, the evidence now points to his authorship of five Christian writings between 512 and 520.

Bonaventure, St. (c. 1217–74)

As a small child, Bonaventure received his name from St. Francis of Assisi* himself when, after being healed through Francis' prayers, the holy friar predicted "good things" (*"buona ventura"*) for him. Bonaventure entered the Franciscan order at age twenty and studied in Paris under the great Alexander of Hales, who praised him for his virtue and brilliance. Later Bonaventure taught alongside St. Thomas Aquinas* in Paris.

In 1257 (at age thirty-six), he was named minister general of the Franciscan order and continued in that post for eighteen years, reconciling divergent groups in the order. Bonaventure presided at the Second Council of Lyons,* which temporarily ended the schism of East and West, but he died toward the end of the council.

Known as the "Seraphic Doctor," Bonaventure was filled with wisdom and charity. His official biography of St. Francis helped unify Francis's followers, and his treatise on *The Soul's Journey into God* became a classic of medieval spirituality. (Feast, July 14.)

Boniface VIII, Pope (c. 1234–1303)

After the abdication of the previous pope, Celestine V, Boniface (elected in 1294) sought to reestablish the dignity and authority of the papacy. Boniface believed in the supreme authority of the papacy both in the spiritual and temporal realms. He was very active in the affairs of European politics, though the majority of his efforts in this regard failed. He also contributed to the improvement of the papal library and archives and added a major section to the Code of Canon law.

In his struggle with French king Philip IV, Boniface declared in *Clericos laicos* (1296) that clergy were exempt from taxation, but backed down when Philip stopped trade with the Vatican. He also canonized Philip's grandfather, King Louis IX.*

Locked in a struggle at home with the powerful Colonna family, Boniface announced the first Jubilee Year in 1300 and granted plenary indulgences to all pilgrims to the apostles'* tombs and basilicas in Rome. This holy year was a tremendous success. Boniface's growing influence emboldened him to issue the bull *Unam Sanctam* in 1302, which asserted the superiority of the pope's spiritual authority over all temporal powers, and concluded that for salvation "every human creature must be subject to the authority of the Roman pontiff." This is the boldest and most far-reaching claim of papal authority in the Church's history.

Ironically, Boniface's papacy ended when he was seized by hostile forces at Anagni in 1303. Though he was rescued by the citizens of Rome, he died a month later from the abuse he had endured. After his pontificate the medieval papacy declined in temporal power and influence.

St. Boniface (c. 680–754)

"The Apostle of Germany," first known as Wynfrith, was born in England around 675 and became a learned monk, publishing a Latin grammar. After Wynfrith's visit to Frisia in 716, God called him to become a missionary. He left England in 718, never to return, and sought approval for his missionary work from Pope Gregory II.* Gregory wrote letters to secure support and cooperation (especially from the Franks) and gave him the name Boniface.

After three difficult years among the Frisians, Boniface returned to Rome in 722 and was consecrated a bishop of the Germanic tribes. Legend has it that when Boniface preached the gospel in the province of Hesse, he won many converts when he cut down a "sacred" tree—the Oak of Thor—and used the wood to build a church.

For the next sixteen years, Boniface continued to preach, baptize, establish churches and monasteries, and train others to assist him. Pope Gregory III made him an archbishop in 732, which meant that Boniface needed to establish sees for bishops under him. After the death of Charles Martel,* Boniface was commissioned to hold a series of synods, held between 740 and 747, to reform the church among the Franks.

This synod was successful, and when Boniface returned to his see of Mainz (in his late seventies), he felt one more missionary call: to return to Frisia, where he had first preached the Gospel. He did so, but was martyred along with his companions by a band of armed pagans in 753. When Boniface's body was buried in the monastery of Fulda, which he had founded, it returned to a Germanic church that was well-organized and firmly established due to his fervor and perseverance. (Feast, June 5.)

Borromeo, St. Charles (1538–84)

Borromeo was one of the great bishops of the Catholic reformation and the guide of the Council of Trent's* third session. Being the nephew of Pope Pius IV, he rose quickly to prominent Church positions while leading a worldly life. But Borromeo changed radically through the *Spiritual Exercises* of St. Ignatius Loyola,* which he took part in around the time of his ordination at age twenty-five.

From that time on, Borromeo's zeal for holiness and reform of the Church was unbounded. He was named cardinal archbishop of Milan in 1561 and played a major role at the final session of Trent (1562–63). He guided the drafting of the *Roman Catechism* and the commission responsible for implementing the Council of Trent in the church.

After the council ended, Borromeo resided in his own diocese of Milan (which was unusual for the archbishop of that time) and undertook a vigorous program of reform and education. He established the Confraternity of Christian Doctrine and founded seven seminaries (including one to train missionary priests for Switzerland) and a new religious congregation (the Oblates of St. Ambrose*) to run them. He also was tireless in caring for the hungry and sick in the famine of 1570 and the plague of 1576–78.

Many resisted his strictly enforced reforms (he was severely wounded by a would-be assassin of the Benedictine order), but he epitomized the new spirit of radical gospel life that swept through the Catholic Church in the mid-to-late sixteenth century. Borromeo was canonized by Pope Pius V in 1610. (Feast, November 4.)

Bosco, St. John (1815–88)

Born into a peasant family near Turin, Italy, Bosco had a vision at age nine that launched his lifelong work of converting and teaching youth. He began with his peers, living a pure and zealous Christian life as a boy, and eventually became a priest in 1841 whose ministry to young people was magnetic.

St. Francis de Sales* was his model. Bosco developed his own educational philosophy based on de Sales, characterized by "reason, religion, and kindness." Indeed, "Don Bosco," as the children called him, was never harsh, exhibiting divine patience and love that affected even the most hardened or hurt young person.

He founded the Salesian order of priests in 1859 and a similar congregation for women with St. Mary Mazzarello in 1872 near Genoa. Don Bosco was innovative, fostering industrial schools and evening classes so that young men could receive practical training in an environment of Catholic faith. Later in life, he also promoted missionary work. He was canonized in 1934, a patron saint of religious educators. (Feast, January 31.)

Bossuet, Jacques (1627–1704)

Bossuet was a luminary of the seventeenth-century French Church as a famous preacher, diplomat, and defender of the Catholic faith. Among his teachers in Paris was St. Vincent de Paul,* and after 1660 his reputation as a preacher grew among the French court. His political influence also grew and, as bishop of Meaux, Bossuet penned the four "Gallican Articles" (1682) and supported the revocation of the Edict of Nantes (1685), which had declared freedom and equality of all religions. He hoped for a peaceful settlement of Christian disunity (as seen in his correspondence with the Protestant philosopher G.W. Leibniz), but he vigorously defended the truth of the Catholic faith.

Bossuet also engaged in a bitter debate with France's other great spiritual guide, Archbishop Francois Fénelon,* which led to the condemnation of Fénelon's teaching as promoting Quietism.* Finally, Bossuet wrote two devotional classics toward the end of his life, *Meditations on the Gospel* (1731) and *Elevation of the Mysteries* (1727).

Brébeuf, St. Jean de (1593–1649)

A tall, rugged French youth, Brébeuf entered the Jesuits in 1617 and was ordained a priest at age twenty-eight in 1622. Three years later, he set off as a missionary to New France (now south-eastern Canada), and with the help of Samuel de Champlain (founder of Quebec), he made the arduous eight-hundred-mile journey inland, by canoe and foot, to the land of the Huron tribe just south of Georgian Bay. He and other "black robes" (Jesuits) began to learn the Huron language and customs but were forced to leave Huronia in 1629 when the French temporarily lost control of the region.

France regained the area in 1632, and Brébeuf returned in 1634, traveling among the people for five years before building the Jesuit mission of Ste. Marie, with Brébeuf appointed as superior. Conversions among the Hurons came slowly, however, as the Jesuits were blamed for smallpox epidemics and Iroquois attacks. Nonetheless, the perseverance of Brébeuf and his companions and their love for the Huron people eventually bore fruit.

Ste. Marie flourished for ten years, until the Iroquois launched a major campaign against the Huron. Brébeuf was brutally tortured and martyred on March 16, 1649. His companions Gabriel Lalement, Charles Garnier, Noel Chabanel, and Antoine Daniel were also martyred, and all (along with St. Issac Jogues* and companions) were canonized by Pope Pius XI in 1930, collectively known as the "North American Martyrs." (Feast, October 19.)

Brethren of the Common Life

A fourteenth-century religious association founded by Gerhard Groote* in the Netherlands, it stressed the practical following of Christ in whatever vocation (lay, clerical, or religious) one belonged to. Its members stressed the importance of education and founded schools throughout the Netherlands and later in Germany. The distinctive spirituality they espoused was known as the *Devotio Moderna*, which was best represented by Thomas* á Kempis in *The Imitation of Christ*.

Besides Kempis, other "Brethren" included Pope Hadrian VI, Gabriel Biel,* Nicholas of Cusa,* and Rudolph Agricola. The "Renaissance" or "New Learning" was encouraged by their focus on education, but their main interest was a deep, personal spirituality that expressed itself in both prayer and action.

Bridget of Sweden, St. (c. 1303–73)

The patron saint of Sweden, Bridget was a wife and the mother of eight children. Her life changed radically after she and her husband, Ulf, made a pilgrimage to Compestella, Spain, in 1341. Thereafter Ulf entered a Cistercian monastery, where he died in 1344, and Bridget also devoted her life to prayer and began to receive revelations.

In these revelations God told her that she was to found a religious community and to urge the pope to move back to Rome from Avignon. With the help of the Cistercians and her daughter, St. Catherine of Sweden, she founded the Brigittine order in 1346. St. Bridget traveled to Rome in the Holy Year of 1350 to seek papal approval for the order, which was granted in 1370.

After 1350, apart from a few pilgrimages, Bridget and her daughter Catherine remained in Rome caring for the poor until her death in 1373 (a few years before the pope's return from Avignon.) She was canonized in 1391, and her visions were published in 1492. (Feast, July 23.)

Brigid, St. (c. 450–525)

Brigid is a legendary Irish saint second only to St. Patrick* in fame. The English word "bride" derives from her name, since the Knights of Chivalry took her as their patroness and called the women they married their "brides" ("brigids"). Her father was a pagan chieftain and her mother a Christian slave.

Raised by a nurse, she worked as a slave for her father, but constantly gave away his goods and food to the poor. A Christian king prevailed upon her father to release Brigid from slavery, which he did. She rejected a marriage arranged by her father and instead embraced the monastic life and founded the first women's religious community in Ireland at Kildare. She and her sisters tirelessly devoted themselves to prayer and charitable works.

While the shamrock is associated with St. Patrick, St. Brigid's symbol was a small cross woven from rushes, which she first wove to explain Christ's passion to a dying pagan. Besides her great charity, Brigid was known as a peacemaker, and many miracles (especially multiplication of food) are said to have accompanied her ministry. (Feast, February 1.)

Bruno, St. (c. 1032–1101)

Bruno was the founder of the Carthusian order, one of the most austere of monastic orders. He was a learned man, named head of the cathedral school in Reims around 1057. The future Pope Urban II* was his student there.

Bruno began his religious life under the capable direction of Robert of Molesme,* founder of Cîteaux (the Cisterians), but soon left with six companions and founded the Carthusian order in 1084 in Grenoble, France, under the protection of the bishop, St. Hugh of Chateanneuf. Pope Urban II called his old mentor to Rome and sought to make Bruno a bishop. Bruno declined, but started another Carthusian monastery in Italy (La Torre), where he died. (Feast, October 6.)

Cabrini, St. Frances Xavier (1850–1917)

Mother Cabrini might be called the "Mother Teresa" of the nineteenth century. A young Italian woman who was so frail that two religious orders rejected her, she finally founded her own order, the Missionary Sisters of the Sacred Heart of Jesus, in 1880. She desired for her missionaries to go to China, but Pope Leo XIII* prevailed upon her to go to the United States to serve the needs of Italian immigrants there.

Mother Cabrini undertook this mission with a loving passion, founding schools, hospitals, and orphanages for the immigrants. These were all staffed by sisters from her religious community, which flourished. Not satisfied with limiting her outreach to the United States, she also established and visited her order in South America and Europe. Despite a fear of water, she sailed across the ocean thirty times to advance the work of her community. She always strove to minister to people with the love of Christ.

Mother Cabrini was a leading educator who advocated holistic education and bilingual education and promoted an "education of the heart" through love, along with the intellect. She died in 1917 in one of her order's hospitals, Columbus Hospital in Chicago. Because she had become a naturalized United States citizen in 1909, she became the first U.S. citizen to be canonized in 1946. Pope Pius XII* also declared her the patron saint of immigrants in 1950. (Feast, November 13.)

Caesarius of Arles, St. (469–542)

Caesarius was the most influential bishop of the Church in sixth-century Gaul. Raised in a wealthy Christian family, he became a monk at age twenty, but illness eventually forced him to return to Arles. He was ordained, became abbot of a local monastery, and was named bishop of Arles in 502.

As a bishop, Caesarius made a tremendous impact on the Church through his preaching (250 of his sermons survive), his foundation of a women's monastery and writing a rule for them, and his presiding at the regional councils of Agde (506) and Orange* (529). (Feast, August 27.)

Callistus, Pope St. (d. c. 222)

His is a remarkable "rags-to-(spiritual) riches" story. Callistus was born a slave and was later sent to the mines of Sardinia. But eventually he was freed and served as a deacon of Rome under Pope Zephyrinus, whom he succeeded as pope in 217.

Callistus saw the Church as embracing both the good and the bad, the "wheat" and the "tares" (see Mt 13:24-30), and thus was accused of moral laxity by the Roman priest Hippolytus.* Eventually, his view of the Church as a refuge of sinners rather than the communion of the "perfect" became accepted as the true Catholic view. He was martyred in 222. The catacombs he administered on the Appian Way today bear his name. (Feast, October 14.)

Calvin, Jean (1509–64)

Calvin, born in Noyon, France, was only eight years old when Martin Luther* posted his "ninety-five theses" on indulgences. At age fourteen Calvin entered the College of Montaigu in Paris, where François Rabelais and Desiderius Erasmus* had studied. He was being prepared for ordination when suddenly his father sent the young Calvin to study law at Orleans. Though he excelled at law, Calvin still considered himself a "humanist" and learned Greek even in the midst of his legal studies.

Calvin was embittered when his father died excommunicated, and so in 1533 or 1534 he was radically converted to Reformation principles. Shortly thereafter (1536) he published the first edition of his major work, *The Institutes of the Christian Religion.*

Calvin became known for personal austerity and strict discipline and for his controversial teaching on predestination. From his native Catholic France, Calvin traveled to Switzerland, first to Basel and then (at the invitation of Guillaume Farel) to Geneva. Even though he was expelled for his extreme views, after three years as a pastor in Strasburg with Martin Bucer, Calvin returned to Geneva and spent most of his later life reforming the city. John Knox, who fled from Scotland to Geneva and later returned to establish Scottish Presbyterianism, called Calvin's Geneva "the most perfect school of Christ since the days of the apostles."

The churches that follow the Calvinist tradition today are known as Reformed or Presbyterian. French Calvinists were known as Huguenots.

Camara, Helder (1909–99)

Archbishop of Olinda and Recife, Brazil, from 1964 until his retirement in the late 1980s, Camara spoke out for the concerns of the poor and fostered non-violent resistance to oppression. His speeches at the Second Vatican* Council contributed to the creation of the *Pastoral Constitution on the Church in the Modern World* (*Gaudium et Spes*).

Campion, St. Edmund (c. 1540–81)

Born in London, Campion was raised Catholic. But he later took the Oath of Supremacy acknowledging Queen Elizabeth as the head of the Church of England and became an Anglican deacon in 1564. Doubts about Protestantism increasingly assailed him, however, and in 1569 he went to Ireland, where further study convinced him that he had been in error. He returned to the Catholic faith.

Forced to flee the persecution unleashed on Catholics when Pope Pius V excommunicated Elizabeth, Campion went to France. There he studied theology, joined the Jesuits, and went to Bohemia the following year for his novitiate. He taught at the college in Prague and in 1578 was ordained there.

Campion and Fr. Robert Parsons were the first Jesuits chosen for the English mission and were sent to England in 1580. His activities among the Catholics—preaching, writing, and administering the sacraments in secret—made him the object of one of the most intensive manhunts in English history. He was betrayed at Lyford, near Oxford, and imprisoned in the Tower of London, but he refused to apostatize when offered rich inducements to do so.

Campion was tortured and then hanged, drawn, and quartered at Tyburn on December 1, 1581, on the technical charge of treason, but in reality because of his priesthood. He was canonized by Pope Paul VI* in 1970 as one of the Forty English and Welsh Martyrs. (Feast, December 1.)

Canisius, St. Peter (1521–97)

The son of the mayor of Nijmegen, the Netherlands, Canisius was born the same year as a young soldier, Ignatius Loyola.* Canisius became one of the most loyal and renowned members of Ignatius' order, the Society of Jesus, which he joined just two years after the rule of the order had been approved by Pope Paul III.* Studying theology at Cologne and Mainz, Canisius was to make his mark as a defender of the Catholic faith against Protestantism.

He published many catechisms, the most influential one appearing in 1555. Four hundred different editions of his catechisms were published over two centuries. Canisius' writing was so persuasive that he is said to have halted the spread of Protestantism in Germany and parts of Austria, and he is known as "the Second Apostle of Germany" (St. Boniface* being the first).

Canisius also helped establish colleges in Munich, Innsbruck, Dillingen, Würzburg, Augsburg, Fribourg, and Vienna. In spite of his renown, he was known by his friends for his simplicity, a strict austerity of life, and a burning love for Jesus Christ. He was the first saint to be canonized and declared a Doctor of the Church at the same time, by Pope Pius XI* in 1925. (Feast, December 21.)

Carroll, John (1735–1815)

John Carroll, whose cousin Charles was the only Catholic signer of the Declaration of Independence, became the first Catholic bishop in America in 1790. He was born in what was then the British colony of Maryland, educated in Flanders, and ordained a Jesuit priest in 1769. However, when the Jesuits were suppressed in 1773, Carroll returned to America and was an active missionary and a valiant patriot in the cause of American independence.

Carroll's friend, Benjamin Franklin, helped convince Pope Pius VI to appoint him the superior of missions in America in 1784, which confirmed the independence of the nation from Britain in the Church's eyes. After his consecration as first U.S. bishop in 1790, Carroll was made archbishop of Baltimore in 1808 as four new sees were created from the original Baltimore diocese, which had encompassed all Catholics in the United States. Carroll's patriotism and leadership served both to promote vigorous growth of the Catholic Church and to secure and defend religious freedom and toleration for Catholics and for all religions in the young republic.

Cassian, St. John (c. 360–435)

Cassian was one of the greatest proponents of monasticism through his life and writings. He emerged in the late fourth century as a monk in Bethlehem who had visited the monasteries in Egypt. His travels took him to Constantinople and Rome, where he was influenced by St. John Chrysostom* and by the future Pope Leo I.* He spent the last fifteen years of his life in Gaul, where he founded monasteries for men and women in Marseilles, and wrote his famous works on monastic life and Christian spirituality: *The Institutes* and *The Conferences*. St. Benedict drew on Cassian's writings in the formulation of his Rule for monks. (Feast, July 23.)

Catacombs

Contrary to popular belief, the catacombs were not hiding places for persecuted Christians or underground churches. They were subterranean cemeteries carved out of the soft but strong tufa stone found in many parts of Italy. The most famous catacombs are those on the roads outside the city walls of Rome, where the early Christians and others buried their dead along the multi-layered labyrinth of tunnels beneath the surface of their property. These were often named after the family who owned the property, though the term "catacombs" was the name of a particular old Roman cemetery located *"Ad Catacumbas"* ("in the sunken valley")— today known as the catacomb of St. Sebastian.

Because of the custom of venerating the remains of martyrs who were buried there, Christians vied to be buried near a martyr. Even after the catacombs were no longer used for burial (by the early fifth century), Christian pilgrims from every part of Europe continued to visit them. Christian symbols and frescoes (portraying Bible stories, the Last Supper, Christians at prayer) adorned the walls of the catacombs, reflecting the Church's faith and hope of eternal life.

When the relics of the martyrs were transferred from the tombs to churches within the city walls early in the ninth century, pilgrimages to the catacombs ceased and the tombs were largely forgotten until the sixteenth century. Today, after exploration and extensive renovation, visitors once more tour the catacombs to catch a glimpse of this important chapter in the Church's journey of faith.

Catherine of Genoa, St. (1447–1510)

As a girl, Catherine Fieschi desired to become a nun but was forced into a marriage that grew increasingly unhappy. Suddenly, in 1473, she had a mystical experience that led to her pursuit of holiness (including daily reception of Holy Communion), and eventually to the conversion of her husband as well. They worked together for twenty years caring for the sick, for which Catherine was declared patroness of Italian hospitals by Pope Pius XII* in 1944.

She also founded a community of lay people pursuing holiness, known as the Oratory of Divine Love, which spread to other cities and later was the model for St. Philip Neri's* famous oratory in Rome. A book published in 1551 contained two writings attributed to her: *Dialogues on the Soul and Body* and *A Treatise on Purgatory*. She died in 1510 after a painful illness and was declared a saint by Pope St. Benedict XIV in 1737. (Feast, September 15.)

Catherine of Siena, St. (1347–80)
Catherine of Siena was named patron saint of Italy, a co-patroness of Europe, and the second female Doctor of the Church (1970) because of her exemplary charity, her deep Christ-centered spirituality, and her courageous conduct and prophetic messages in the midst of two of the Catholic Church's greatest trials in her history. These accomplishments are amazing for one who, like Christ, had no formal training in theology and died at age thirty-three!

Catherine was the twenty-third of twenty-five children, and from her youth she exhibited great love for God, expressed in intense prayer and mortification. Her parents misunderstood her, refusing her entrance into religious life and insisting that she marry. After a time they relented, and Catherine lived at home as a third order (lay) Dominican. When she was sixteen, God called her to go out and care for the sick and the poor.

Catherine soon became known for her extraordinary wisdom, and many followed her as she traveled, often helping make peace between towns and warring factions. Once she was called upon to heal a breach between Florence and the Holy See. She had a prophetic sense that the pope, residing in Avignon, must return to Rome. Her audiences with Pope Gregory XI* contributed to his move back to Rome in 1377.

Tragically, the Great Schism* began the year after his return. Catherine wrote and spoke on behalf of Pope Urban VI* as the true pope, but the tension and grief caused by the schism may have contributed to her death in Rome in 1380.

Catherine was a mystic who also possessed an invisible stigmata. Her *Dialogues* are among the great classics of Catholic spirituality, emphasizing the love of Christ as revealed in his passion and crucifixion, and symbolized by his blood shed for the salvation of the world. Also preserved of her writings are sixteen prayers and 383 letters. (Feast, April 29.)

Cecilia, St. (second or third century)
Although many varying legends surround her, it is thought that this noble Roman lady suffered martyrdom under the Roman emperor Marcus Aurelius. Images venerating her death show her head partially severed, after attempts to suffocate her with hot vapors failed. She is the patron saint of sacred music and musicians because of her storied musical accomplishments and singing of psalms at her wedding.

In the catacombs of Pope St. Callistus* there is an image of St.

Cecilia with her hands held aloft in praise (the *orans* or praying posture commonly used when worshipping God in the early Church.) She epitomizes St. Augustine's* celebrated saying, "One who sings prays twice." (Feast, November 22.)

Cerularius, Michael (d. 1058)

The Great Schism* of the Church into Orthodox (Eastern) and Catholic (Western) bodies occurred during Cerularius' reign as patriarch of Constantinople (1043–58). His strongly anti-Latin outlook led him to turn a deaf ear to a papal delegation led by Cardinal Humbert of Silva-Candida.* The frustrated Humbert finally laid a bull excommunicating Cerularius on the altar of his church (Hagia Sophia).

The patriarch responded by issuing anathemas against Humbert and the Latin Church in 1054. Four years later, Cerularius was removed from office by Emperor Isaac Comnenus, leaving the tragic division of the Church unreconciled.

Chalcedon, Council of (451)

This fourth ecumenical (that is, universal) council of the Church was called in 451 by the Emperor Marcian to settle the "Christological controversy" that had come to a head in the mid-fifth century. Two years before Chalcedon, the so-called "Robber Council" of Ephesus (449) had accepted the doctrinal formula of the monk Eutyches* that Jesus possessed "one nature [that is, the divine] after the union" of his divine and human natures—that is, after the Incarnation. The political maneuvering of Dioscorus,* patriarch (archbishop) of Alexandria, secured the "Robber Council's" success and the deposition of his rival, Flavian, patriarch of Constantinople.

Nevertheless, the decisions of the council in 449 were reversed by the Council of Chalcedon, which declared that Jesus Christ is "one Person in two natures" that exist in Christ "without confusion or change, without division or separation." This was accepted as the Church's faith at this universal council. However, some Christians, called Monophysites (from the Greek words for "one nature"), rejected this council's teaching and went into schism, thinking that Chalcedon compromised Christ's divinity.

This group, which followed the teaching of Dioscorus and Eutyches, grew to their greatest influence in the mid-sixth century. Meanwhile, the Council of Chalcedon provided the unifying standard of understanding and language to describe the union of the divine and human natures of Christ (called the "hypostatic union") in one Person.

Chantal, St. Jeanne François de (1572–1641)

Born into a noble family, Jeanne (or Jane) married a wealthy baron in 1592 and bore four children. After nine years of marriage, she was widowed and decided to live as a celibate. Coming under the spiritual direction of St. Francis de Sales* in 1604, with his help and encouragement she founded a religious community, the Congregation of the Visitation, for young girls and widows who desired to serve God through active life in the world.

With her sisters, Jeanne devoted herself to charitable works, serving the sick and the poor. By the time of her death in 1641, she had founded eighty-six houses of Visitation sisters. St. Vincent de Paul* attested to her radical holiness, and she has been recognized as a leader of the Catholic Reformation. Jeanne was canonized in 1767. (Feast, August 21.)

Charlemagne (c. 742–814)

Charlemagne ("Charles the Great") has been called the "new Constantine." He and his brother Carloman succeeded his father Pepin* (Pippin) III as rulers of the Kingdom of the Franks in 768. Charles became sole ruler upon his brother's death in 771 and ruled until 814. He was a conqueror, at war forty-two of the forty-three years of his reign, and gave the conquered peoples the choice to be baptized "by water or by blood."

Charlemagne defended Rome from the Lombard invasion, and when he visited Rome in 800, Pope Leo III crowned him "Emperor of the Romans." This was the beginning of the "Holy Roman Empire" of the Middle Ages, a manifestation of "Christendom"—an alliance of the Church and state. His capital was Aachen, where today still stands his impressive Romanesque cathedral church.

While Charlemagne was in power, there was no question about who was the head of this Church-state union. Charlemagne wrote to Pope Leo III that it was the emperor's duty to rule Christendom, and the pope's task to pray for it. Charlemagne exercised his assumed authority by practicing "lay investiture," the selection and appointing of clergy by the state. He also became involved in theological issues, opposing the heresies of adoptionism and iconoclasm, and insisting that the *filioque* clause (affirming that the Holy Spirit proceeds from both the Father "and the Son") be included in the Nicene-Constantinopolitan Creed.*

Although himself practically illiterate, Charlemagne realized the importance of education. He insisted that there be schools attached to every cathedral and monastery for the education of the nobility. He encouraged the copying of ancient manuscripts and appointed the monk Alcuin* to be his "minister of education." His biographer, Einhard, was also a scholar of considerable repute. This rebirth of learning under Charlemagne is known as the "Carolingian Renaissance."

Not every one of his endeavors was successful, however. Charlemagne's forces could not drive the Moors out of Spain; the heroic epic poem, "The Song of Roland," enshrines one of their defeats. Charlemagne's legacy was a politically unified Western Europe loyal to the Catholic faith and the pope. Even though the Holy Roman Empire began to disintegrate under his sons, Christendom continued to be the ideal of the government throughout the Middle Ages, with the Catholic faith its animating principle.

Chesterton, G.K. (1874-1936)

A brilliant literary and social critic, Chesterton left the Church of England in 1922 to become a Catholic. As a Catholic, he turned his wit and literary talent to apologies for the Catholic Church (*The Catholic Church and Conversion*, 1926), biographies of St. Francis of Assisi* (1923) and St.

Thomas Aquinas* (1933), and other influential works, such as *The Everlasting Man* (1925) and his *Autobiography* (1936). He also wrote the "Fr. Brown" detective stories, which frequently convey moral lessons. Chesterton was given the title "Defender of the Catholic Faith" by Pope Pius XI.*

Clare, St. (1194-1253)

One of the first to follow the example of St. Francis of Assisi,* Clare became the foundress of the "Second Order" of St. Francis, the "Poor Clares." Her family opposed Clare's aspiration to a poor, celibate life, but she persevered and eventually was joined by two of her own sisters and her widowed mother. The Church of San Damiano, which Francis had repaired himself, became the mother house of Clare's order. She also wrote a rule for the community—stricter than the Benedictine rule—which was given final approval by Pope Innocent IV two days before her death in 1253. She was canonized in 1255. (Feast, August 11.)

Clement I of Rome, St. (d. c. 99)

Clement was the third bishop of Rome after St. Peter. He is listed by St. Irenaeus* as succeeding St. Linus and St. Cletus in the chair (office) of Peter. We know of him through a letter he wrote to the church in Corinth about the year 96.

With apostolic authority, he admonished a group of young men who were seeking to overthrow the established elders, thus threatening to create a schism (division) in the church. Clement joined with other apostolic fathers* in this era in stressing the importance of Church unity and respect for the established elders. There is no sharp distinction in his writings between the "bishops" (*episcopoi*) and "elders" (*presbyteroi*); hence the leadership pattern (hierarchy) of the local churches was still developing. His other pastoral advice to the church is similar to that of St. Paul's epistles.

One of the earliest preserved Christian homilies is called the *Second Letter of Clement*, but its style indicates that Clement was not its author. (Feast, November 23.)

Clement V, Pope (1264–1314)

Clement was archbishop of Bordeaux when elected pope in 1305, still in the shadow of Pope Boniface VIII,* who had battled with the French king Philip IV. This intelligent but indecisive Frenchman gave in to the pressure of Philip, first to create nine new French cardinals in 1305, and later to move the see of Peter from Rome to Avignon in southern France in 1309—

the beginning of what has been called the "Babylonian Captivity of the Church." This was only the beginning: Clement was forced to absolve from all guilt (and even to praise) all those Frenchmen (from the king down) who were responsible for the shameful imprisonment of Boniface VIII.

In return for the king's withdrawal of a demand for a posthumous trial of Boniface, Clement agreed to suppress the Knights Templar, allowing their leaders to be tortured until they confessed to criminal activity. Clement had their vast wealth (earmarked for the Knights Hospitaller) turned over to Philip. These actions were confirmed at the Council of Vienne (1311–12), the fifteenth ecumenical council of the Catholic Church.

There were instances in which Clement acted independently of French interests, such as when he settled the dispute between the Franciscans and their spiritual offshoot, founded the universities at Orleans and Perugia, and established programs of Oriental languages at four universities to promote missionary work.

Clement XIV, Pope (1705–74)

The reign of Clement XIV (1769–74) marks a nadir of the papacy as he succumbed to political pressure (especially from France and Spain) and ordered the suppression of the largest Catholic religious order, the Society of Jesus (Jesuits), in all Catholic states in 1773. This concession did not satisfy the opponents of the papacy, who used the weakness of Clement as an opportunity for further infringements on the Church's rights in their territories.

Clement of Alexandria, St.
(c. 150–c. 215)

Clement was a convert to Christianity whose philosophical quest led him from his native Athens to many cities. He settled in Alexandria, Egypt, where he studied under the famous Christian leader Pantaenus. Gnosticism* was the prevalent philosophy there, and Clement boldly asserted that the true *gnosis* (knowledge) which brings freedom and salvation is revealed by God in Jesus Christ.

Clement's three most noted works are the evangelistic *Protrepticus (Exhortation to the Greeks)*; the instructional work *Paedagogus* (*The Tutor*), and *Stromateis* (*Miscellanies*), an unsystematic survey of Christian teaching and philosophy.

Clement fled Alexandria in the persecution of Septimus Serverus in 203, and Origen* later succeeded him as Alexandria's most prominent Christian teacher. Clement died in Cappadocia somewhere between 211 and 216. He is best remembered as developing the first Christian "philosophy of religion."

Clovis (c. 466–511) and Clotilda (474–545)

Clotilda, princess of Burgundy, was a fervent Catholic whose prayers contributed to the conversion of her husband, Clovis, to the Catholic faith. Clovis, the warrior-king of the Franks, initially resisted Christianity but later viewed his improbable victory over the Alemanni when he prayed to his wife's God as a sign that he should become a Catholic. The bishop of Rheims, St. Remigius, baptized Clovis along with three thousand of his subjects in 496.

Clovis then defeated the Arian* king of the Visigoths, Alaric II, and continued to spread the Catholic faith "by the sword"—by conquest. His biographer, St. Gregory of Tours,* portrayed Clovis as a "new Constantine" whose dynasty (the Merovingian dynasty) laid the foundations for Catholic medieval France. He divided his united kingdom among his sons at his death, while his wife Clotilda entered the convent of St. Martin of Tours* and became known for her holiness.

Cluny

The renewal of monastic life began in the tenth century at the Benedictine abbey of Cluny in the Burgundy region of France. Duke William of Aquitaine founded the monastery in 910 with St. Berno as its first abbot. Cluny became the model of fervent religious life for many other abbeys.

St. Odo became abbot in 927, and in a visit to Rome in 936 he caused several Italian monasteries (including Monte Cassino, Benedict's own foundation) to follow Cluniac principles. St. Odilo, Cluny's fifth abbot (994–1049), increased the number of monasteries affiliated with Cluny (from thirty-seven to sixty-five) and formed them into a monastic order under the authority of the abbot of Cluny. He also established the Feast of All Souls on November 2 and worked for a day of peace, the "Truce of God," in southern France and Italy.

St. Hugh, who succeeded him, had a magnificent church built at Cluny, which was the largest Christian church building before St. Peter's in Rome. Under Hugh (abbot 1049–1109), the height of Cluny's influence was reached, with over a thousand Cluniac houses flourishing across Europe.

Columba of Iona, St. (c. 521–97)

The son of an Irish prince, Columba studied at the monastic school of St. Finnian. After his ordination Columba preached and founded monasteries throughout Ireland. His most famous monastery was at Iona, founded in 563 off the west coast of Scotland.

This island became the center of evangelization by these Irish monk-missionaries to other islands, to Scotland (which was named after the Irish, who were called *scoti* in those days), and later to northern England. Besides the gospel, these monks brought with them a rich culture of music, poetry, sculpture, and illuminated manuscripts. In his later life, Columba was known as a scholar, poet, and peacemaker, befitting his name, which means "dove." (Feast, June 9.)

Columban(us), St. (c. 543–615)

A monk and a missionary, Columban began his greatest work when he left his Irish monastery home in 590 and set out for Gaul. There he preached, corrected abuses, and founded monasteries in Burgundy at Annegray and Luxeuil. He also introduced the Irish practice of private confession to mainland Europe.

Columban was outspoken and persistent in condemning laxity both in common people and rulers. He and his monks were driven from his monastery around 610 for rebuking the king. They traveled in exile through Gaul and Germany, preaching and founding monasteries as they went, until they settled and founded a monastery at Bobbio in Italy.

Columban died around 615. He left behind a vibrant message of repentance and renewal wherever he had traveled, as well as many writings: letters, homilies, a monastic rule, a penitential discipline, and some vivid poetry. (Feast, November 23.)

Congar, (Marie-Joseph) Yves (1904–95)

A French Dominican priest, Congar pioneered the work of ecumenism (*Divided Christendom*, 1937, was a major work), tradition and the theology of the laity. He was an influential *peritus* (expert) at the Second Vatican* Council. He authored *True and False Renewal in the Church, Tradition and Traditions*, and in his later years, the three-volume *I Believe in the Holy Spirit*. Pope John Paul II* declared Congar a cardinal in 1994, shortly before his death in 1995.

Constance, Council of (1414–17)

This council, the sixteenth ecumenical council of the Catholic Church, ended the Great Schism* of three claimants to the papacy within the Catholic Church. The supporters of the "conciliar theory" proposed that an ecumenical council's authority was greater than that of the papacy, and that a council could be called without the pope in case of dire necessity.

The emperor Sigismund convinced the anti-pope John XXIII to call this council to end the Great Schism. In 1414, the council was convened, but John tried to flee the city secretly after it was decided that the voting would be counted by nation and not by individual bishop. In the end, Pope Martin V was elected and the other papal claimants, including the legitimate pope in office, Gregory XII, eventually stepped aside.

The council also passed decrees calling for frequent ecumenical councils (*Frequens*) and declaring the superior authority of the ecumenical council over all Catholics, even the pope (in *Sacrosancta*). However, the Catholic Church never held frequent ecumenical councils, and later judged that an ecumenical council must be held with the pope's leadership (or at least recognition), though in an "emergency" (as at Constance) it could begin without the pope's consent. This council also condemned teachings of John Wycliff* and Jan Huss,* and ordered that Huss be burned as a heretic.

Constantine the Great (d. 337)

The most significant political event for Christianity in the first millennium was the ascendancy of Constantine as Roman Emperor in 312. In that year, he issued (with the Eastern emperor Licinius) the Edict of Milan, which legalized Christianity and ended three centuries of sporadic government persecution of Christians.

Constantine attributed his dramatic victory in 312 over Maxentius at the battle of the Milvian Bridge to the Christian God. Though he was not baptized until shortly before his death in 337, Constantine was a catechumen and acted throughout his reign as a patron of Christianity. He built churches, prohibited violent entertainment and the branding of slaves, made Sunday a day of rest by closing government businesses and courts, and restored to Christians confiscated goods and property. He raised his children as Christians so that this heritage would be carried on after his death.

The implications of this religious turnabout were vast. Many in the empire flocked to the Church, seeing that the political and social climate now favored this move, and so the Church had to deal with an influx of catechumens. When the teaching of Arius* threatened to divide the Church, Constantine took it upon himself to call all the bishops together at Nicea* in 325 to settle the matter.

Tragically, Bishop Eusebius of Nicomedia later convinced the emperor that Nicea had made a mistake in condemning Arius, and so he (and his sons later) began to exile pro-Nicea bishops, such as St. Athanasius of Alexandria.* Thus, the emergence of "Christendom" (the unity of the Catholic Church and the state) presaged even in Constantine's rule the problems of delineating the proper spheres of secular and Church authority, as well as raising the concern about the spiritual vitality of a Church with increasing numbers of converts for social and political reasons. Christianity, so long a counterculture in a pagan society, was now forming a culture that was to reign in Europe for the next thousand years.

Constantinople, First Council of (381)

Recognized as the second ecumenical council of the Catholic Church, this council reaffirmed the Council of Nicea's* condemnation of Arius* and asserted the full divinity of the Holy Spirit (against the Macedonians or *Pneumatomachi*) as well. The creed* of this council (commonly called the Nicene Creed, but more properly the Niceno-Constantinopolitan Creed) expressed these beliefs, and has been the official creed of the Greek Church and also of the Latin West (with the later addition of the *filioque* clause) up to the present time.

This council also decreed that the see of Constantinople was second only to Rome in dignity and authority. But Rome refused to accept the canon (number three) because it was offensive to certain churches, particularly to Alexandria and Antioch, which had been prominent long before the emperors had ruled from Constantinople.

Constantinople, Second Council of (553)

This council, counted as the fifth ecumenical council of the Catholic Church, was called by the emperor Justinian* in response to continued confusion about the union of the divine and human natures in Christ and how he saves us. The council reaffirmed the condemnation of Nestorianism* (that is, the belief that Mary could not be called *Theotokos*, "mother of God"), and also condemned some writings (called the *Three Chapters*) of Theodore of Mopsuestia,* Theodore of Cyprus, and Ibas of Edessa.

Constantinople, Third Council of (680–81)

This sixth ecumenical council of the Catholic Church condemned the Monothelite heresy, which claims that while on earth Jesus possessed only one will—the divine will. The council clarified that because Jesus possessed a perfectly united divine and human nature, he also possessed (and now possesses in glory) a fully unified divine will and human will.

Contarini, Gasparo (1483–1542)

Contarini was a Venetian who served as a diplomat for Venice but was made a cardinal by Pope Paul III* in 1535, when he was fifty-two. He was also an excellent theologian who had written against Martin Luther,* but as cardinal he arranged a meeting with Luther to seek reconciliation and perhaps even some doctrinal agreement. This meeting—the Colloquy of Ratisbon in 1541—did achieve some significant breakthroughs, but the agreements reached there were subsequently rejected by leadership of both sides. Disillusioned by this failure and even accused of heresy, Contarini died in 1542, ending any hope of a reconciliation between Catholics and Lutherans.

Copernicus, Nicolas (1473–1543)
A Polish scholar and astronomer (1415–1543), Copernicus taught the theory that the planets of the solar system revolve around the sun rather than the earth (as Ptolemy had taught). His ideas formed the basis of modern astronomy. Later, the Italian Galileo Galilei* confirmed Copernicus' theory through observation, which precipitated a controversy in the Church in the sixteenth century.

Creeds
Short doctrinal summaries or "rules of faith" were formulated in local churches beginning in the first and second centuries to be professed by those who were to be baptized. From the earliest profession that "Jesus is Lord" (see Phil 2:11; 1 Cor 12:3), these creeds soon included statements of belief in the Trinity (see Mt 28:19) and in Jesus' death and resurrection.

Eventually the creeds were authorized by the bishops and written down. These "local" creeds were succeeded by the Apostles' Creed* in the West and by the Nicene Creed (from the Council of Nicea,* 325, revised to its present form by the Council of Constantinople* in 381) in the East, beginning in the fourth century. In the East the Nicene Creed began to be recited at Mass during the fifth century.

The profession of the creeds promoted the unity of the Church's faith and helped to refute heresies such as Gnosticism.*

Crusades
First Crusade
Pope Urban II* launched this endeavor at the Council of Clermont in 1095. Its purpose was to assist the Byzantine Church, which was being oppressed with the ascendancy of the Seljuk Turks, and to free the city of Jerusalem from control of these Turks, who were limiting or forbidding Christian pilgrimages to the holy sites.

Those who went on the crusade were promised protection of their property, a plenary indulgence, and the reward of martyrdom if they died in battle. Armies from across Europe, led by Raymond of Toulouse, Godfrey of Bouillon, Robert of Normandy, Behemond and Tancred of Apulia, and Bishop Adhemar of LePuy, gathered in Constantinople and proceeded to take Antioch (1098) and Jerusalem (1099). The Latin Kingdom of Jerusalem was established, with Godfrey of Bouillon as its first ruler, and his brother Baldwin succeeding him (crowned Christmas Day, 1100). Other Latin "Crusader States" (Antioch, Tripoli, Jerusalem, and Edessa) were established to maintain access for Christian pilgrims to the holy places.

The crusade also opened new trade with the East. Tragically, some of the warriors did engage in the crusades out of mercenary motives, or for worldly glory and power. The excessive shedding of Muslim blood by the crusaders in Jerusalem and in other battles has been a source of scandal and shame. At the time, though, the First Crusade was seen by most European Christians as a great success, having freed the Holy Land from hostile control and allowing pilgrimages to the sacred sites to continue.

Second Crusade

In 1147 the city of Edessa, a small Latin Crusader state, fell to Muslim forces, provoking Pope Eugene III to proclaim a second crusade to defend the other crusader states. Preached by St. Bernard of Clairvaux,* this crusade was a massive effort led by King Louis VII of France and Conrad III of Germany. But it turned out to be a total military failure and marked the beginning of the decline of the crusading movement.

Third Crusade

This "King's Crusade" (1189–92) was a response to Saladin's capture of Jerusalem in 1187. Emperor Frederick I Barbarossa, Richard the Lionhearted of England, and Philip II Augustus of France planned to join forces to retake the Holy City. Frederick died on the journey, and Richard and Philip captured the coastal city of Acre—but only after two years of fighting and loss of the lives of as many as a hundred thousand crusaders.

When Philip and Richard quarreled, Richard was left to fight Saladin alone. He achieved a partial victory—a treaty that allowed Christian pilgrims to enter Jerusalem—but the city remained in Saladin's control. During Richard's return journey to England, he was captured and had to be ransomed from the castle of Durnstein on the Danube.

Fourth Crusade

This crusade, launched in 1204, was originally intended to aid the Holy Land by an attack against Egypt. But through the influence of the Venetians (who were supplying the fleet) and the French, the crusade was diverted to Constantinople. There the crusaders mercilessly sacked the city and established a Latin kingdom.

Though this action temporarily united the Eastern and Western churches by force (through the establishment of a Latin patriarch in Constantinople), the long-term effect was to deepen the bitterness of the Orthodox toward the West and to prolong the schism. Pope Innocent III* denounced the misdirection of the crusade and excommunicated some of its leaders, but he did recognize the Latin patriarchate.

Fifth Crusade

This crusade, launched in 1218 and carried out under Pope Honorius III (pope 1216–27), targeted Egypt and succeeded in capturing Damietta in 1219. The crusade might have been further successful, but the failure of Emperor Frederick II to arrive with reinforcements and the weak leadership of Cardinal Pelagius led to a mere truce after the loss of thousands of crusader lives.

Sixth Crusade

Although excommunicated by Pope Gregory IX* for procrastinating in initiating this crusade, Emperor Frederick II finally undertook it in 1228 and brilliantly negotiated Christian control of Jerusalem, Bethlehem, and Nazareth. Frederick was crowned King of Jerusalem in 1229, but after his departure the Latin empire weakened, and Jerusalem fell to the Muslims in 1244, never to be regained.

Seventh Crusade

Responding to Pope Innocent IV's lament over the fall of Jerusalem in 1244, King (St.) Louis IX of France* led this crusade in 1248, focusing attention on Egypt. The army of forty or fifty thousand troops captured Damietta, but thereafter was reduced in battle to six thousand men, who were eventually captured and ransomed. Louis remained in the East, seeking to secure the aid of the Mongols, but failed and returned to France in 1254 upon the death of his mother.

Eighth Crusade

The eighth and final major crusade, led by King St. Louis IX* of France and Charles of Anjou, was initiated to defend Christian territories against the fierce Malemukes led by the sultan Baybars. After he took Antioch in 1268, King Louis laid siege to Tunis, where he (with his son) died in 1270.

Charles of Anjou took command but retreated and sailed home instead of fighting. The Malemukes proceeded to capture Christian strongholds one by one over the next twenty years. The fall of Acre, the last Christian stronghold, in 1291 marks the end of the crusader era.

Although the crusades proved in the end to be military failures, they opened trade with the East and brought the West into contact with cultural treasures such as the writings of Aristotle. Tragically, the crusaders' sack of Constantinople in 1204 and other atrocities deepened the animosity of many Eastern (Orthodox) Christians against the Latin West and have prolonged the schism of the Church.

Cursillo

Cursillo is Spanish for "short course." This Catholic movement was founded in 1945 by Bishop Hervas Benet and a group of lay people in Mallorca, Spain, who sought to renew the vision and fervor of Catholics for living the gospel daily in joy and power. Though it began in Spain, it became popular in many Spanish-speaking countries and communities in the Western Hemisphere.

On weekend retreats, Cursillo leaders present a "short course" in Christianity designed to promote conversion (or deeper conversion) to Christ, and then to support and spread this spirit through regular small group meetings of committed *cursillistas*. The Cursillo was inspired by the *Spiritual Exercises* of St. Ignatius of Loyola.* Many *cursillistas* have become involved in other Catholic renewal movements, notably the Catholic charismatic renewal.

Cyprian of Carthage, St. (d. 258)

It was a notable event in ancient Carthage when, in the year 246, the prominent civic leader Cyprian converted to Christianity and was baptized. Within a year he was ordained a priest and then raised to the episcopal office in 248 or 249. As a bishop, he worked with Pope St. Cornelius (251–53) to counter the schism of Novatian,* who denied the authority of the Church to forgive serious sins (such as murder, adultery, and apostasy).

Soon the great persecution by the emperor Decius* raged, and Cyprian guided his flock through letters while in hiding. Pope Cornelius died in the persecution and was succeeded by Pope Stephen I. After touting the papacy as the guarantor of the Church's oneness in his great treatise, *On the Unity of the Catholic Church,* Cyprian was shocked to learn that Stephen held that baptism administered in proper form by heretics or schismatics was valid. In Cyprian's view, nothing done outside of the unity of the one, holy, catholic, and apostolic church could be valid.

He argued with Stephen and asserted the right of the bishops to teach the truth in unity, even without the bishop of Rome. Before this disagreement erupted into an open breach, the renewal of persecution by the emperor

Valerian led to the martyrdom of both Stephen and Cyprian. Cyprian, the first North African bishop to die for his faith, shares a feast day with his friend and fellow martyr, Pope St. Cornelius (September 16.)

Cyril, St. (826–69) and Methodius, St. (c. 815–85)

Called "the Apostles of the Slavic People," these two brothers were declared copatrons of Europe (along with St. Benedict*) by Pope John Paul II* in 1980. His fourth encyclical letter, *Slavorum Apostoli* (June 2, 1985) is dedicated to them.

Born in a Greek city (Salonika) on the border of Slavic territory in the early ninth century, Methodius, the elder of the two, was a civil official until he entered a monastery at the foot of Mount Olympus. His brother, Constantine (now known by his religious name, Cyril) was a brilliant student in the capital, where he turned down a political career to become a priest. He served in some important posts until retiring to a monastery. Cyril was called back to Constantinople and served as a teacher (earning the title "the Philosopher") and then as a delegate to the Saracens for the emperor and the patriarch.

At this point, the brothers were united in service. They were sent to the Crimea, where they discovered the bones of Pope St. Clement I,* which they solemnly presented to Pope Hadrian II.

Their greatest work began when Prince Ratislav of Moravia asked Emperor Michael III to send him missionaries to explain Christianity in their language. Cyril and Methodius arrived in 863 and translated the liturgy into Old Slavonic, using the Slavonic (or Cyrillic) alphabet devised by St. Cyril. They celebrated this liturgy with Prince Kocel in Nitra and returned with him to Rome to get the pope's approval. Pope Hadrian II greeted them and approved their work, but Cyril died there on February 14, 869.

Methodius was appointed archbishop of Pannonia (Moravia), and despite jealousy and opposition from Latin bishops, he tirelessly continued his apostolic work. The pope continued to defend Methodius and his ministry from the attacks of some narrow-minded bishops, as did the Byzantine patriarch and the emperor.

These two brothers, Cyril and Methodius, exemplify the unity of the Catholic cultures of East and West, as well as missionary zeal. As Pope John Paul II* has written of them, their "effort to learn the language and to understand the mentality of the new peoples ... make Cyril and Methodius true models for all [the] missionaries" (*Slavorum Apostoli*, no. 11). (Feast, February 14.)

Cyril of Alexandria, St. (378–444)
Though he was one of the greatest teachers of the true meaning of Jesus Christ's divinity, little is known about St. Cyril before mention is made of him at the Council of the Oak in 403. As successor of Theophilus as patriarch of Alexandria in 412, Cyril was immediately thrown into the controversies of his day. He quietly restored honor to the memory of St. John Chrysostom* (whom the Council of the Oak had condemned), and soon took on his greatest theological opponent, Nestorius.*

Following the tradition of the Church, Cyril insisted that the Blessed Virgin Mary be honored with the title *Theotokos* ("God-bearer" or "Mother of God"). This teaching was adopted by the First Council of Ephesus in 431, which condemned the Nestorian heresy. Cyril's Marian theology was based on his understanding of Jesus Christ as the eternal Word of God who united himself fully (in his *hypostasis*—the closest possible union) to "flesh enlivened by a rational soul."

Thus, Cyril proclaimed belief in Christ's full humanity as well as his divinity. Cyril's emphasis on Jesus' divinity was deeply rooted in the thought of the great Alexandrine theologians, especially St. Athanasius.* Six years after Cyril's death, his theology was a crucial component of the Council of Chalcedon's* Christological definition, and also of the teaching of the Second Council of Constantinople* in 553.

Cyril was a powerful and controversial figure. He is sometimes blamed for the murder of the Neo-Platonic philosopher Hypatia by a Christian mob in 415, but there is no evidence that he was responsible. Because of his profound theological insight and extensive writings, Cyril is ranked among the great figures of his era (with Origen,* Athanasius,* the Cappadocians, and Augustine*) and was given the title "Seal of All the Fathers." (Feast, June 27.)

Cyril of Jerusalem, St. (c. 315–86)
Although little is known of Cyril's background, he is acclaimed for his catechetical lectures preparing those to be baptized (the *photizomenoi*) for their "enlightenment" or "illumination" through the sacraments. These homilies, presented during Lent and Easter of the years 348–50, review the creed* and main points of Catholic doctrine before Easter (*procatechesis*). Then, after Easter, they present a

detailed explanation of the meaning of the sacraments that had just been received (mystagogical catechesis). These teachings have been valuable in recent times for the Church's restoration of the Rite of Christian Initiation of Adults (RCIA). Cyril continued as bishop of Jerusalem until his death in about 386. (Feast, March 18.)

Damasus I, Pope St. (c. 304–84)

Pope from 366 to 384, Damasus is remembered most for commissioning St. Jerome* to translate the Bible from the original languages into Latin—the "Vulgate" ("common") Bible. He also adorned the tombs of martyrs of Rome with epitaphs (many that he composed himself) engraved in marble.

He presided over the Council of Rome in 382, which confirmed the teaching of the First Council of Constantinople* of 381 (condemning the Arians* and the *pneumatomachi* or Macedonians, who denied the divinity of the Holy Spirit). The document promulgating the decrees of that council is known as the *Tome of Damasus*. (Feast, December 11.)

Damian, St. Peter (1007–72)

An austere monk and eloquent preacher, Damian exemplifies the zealous pursuit of Church reform, especially reform of the clergy, in the eleventh century. His renown began in the 1040s as a leader, reformer, and founder of Benedictine monasteries in Italy. He was tireless in writing and preaching against the abuses he saw.

Reluctantly he accepted the office of cardinal bishop of Ostia in 1057, but he used this office to continue and intensify his work of reform. He was also wise and moderate, as when he recognized sacraments administered by simoniacal clergy as valid. Damian was pronounced a Doctor of the Church by Pope Leo XII in 1828. (Feast, February 21.)

da Vinci, Leonardo (1452–1519)

Leonardo was not only a famous Italian Renaissance painter (creator of *The Last Supper, Mona Lisa,* and *St. John the Baptist*); he was also a scholar and a scientist, contributing to geology, weapon making, and even fanciful, futuristic aircraft designs. He died in France in 1519.

Day, Servant of God Dorothy (1897–1980)

Born into a non-religious home in upstate New York, Dorothy Day spent most of her adolescent and young adult years searching for truth. In her twenties she was a journalist for several socialist newspapers. When she had a child out of wedlock, her desire for the child to be baptized resulted ultimately in her conversion to Catholicism.

Day met a staunch Catholic, Peter Maurin, who worked with her to found a newspaper, *The Catholic Worker*, devoted to promoting Catholic social teaching. She also founded hospitality houses for the poor in several major cities. Until her death in 1980, Day worked tirelessly, speaking out for peace, the value of the person, and social justice. Her cause for canonization was opened in 2000, when she was declared a Servant of God.

Decian Persecution

The infamous Roman emperor Decius (ruled 249–51) is remembered by Christians as launching the first organized empire-wide persecution of the Church. Christians had been scapegoats before, but Decius blamed the increasing problems of the whole empire on their refusal to worship the gods of Rome. He demanded that each Christian pay homage and receive a letter (*libellus*) to certify that they had done so, or else face imprisonment or death.

Many Christians were martyred, but many more (called the "lapsed") offered sacrifice or paid a bribe to receive a letter—committing the sin of apostasy (denying the faith). This raised the question of whether or how the lapsed could later be forgiven or reconciled to the Church.

The Decian persecution served as a "wake-up call" to Christians who had not experienced persecution and were weak in their faith. When Valerian (emperor 253–60) renewed the persecution at the end of his reign, he found the Church stronger and better prepared. The edict of toleration issued by the emperor Gallienus in 260 ended the period of Christian persecution by Decius and Valerian and ushered in forty years of relative peace for the Church.

de Lubac, Henri (1896–1991)

This French Jesuit theologian was among those who sought to renew Catholic theology in the twentieth century by returning to the patristic sources of Catholic faith. To this end, he cofounded *Sources Chrétiennes*, a series of patristic texts and translations. His first major work was *Surnaturel*, which corrected false distinctions between the "natural" and the "supernatural" orders that had been promoted by some neo-Scholastic theologies.

De Lubac was a *peritus* (expert) at the Second Vatican* Council, and authored (in English translation), *The Mystery of the Supernatural* (1967), *The Splendor of the Church* (1956, 1986), *Catholicism: A Study of the Corporate Destiny of Mankind* (1950). He was named a cardinal by Pope John Paul II* shortly before his death in 1991.

de Paul, St. Vincent (c. 1580–1660)
Today Vincent de Paul is a familiar name because of the charitable organization that its founder, Blessed Frederick Ozanam, named after him in 1833. In his own day, Vincent was also well known for his charity and was regarded by many as the "conscience of France." Seeds of this vocation were planted when, as a young priest, he was captured by pirates and held captive until he escaped after two years, in 1607.

Cardinal Pierre de Bérulle* counseled Vincent to devote his priestly ministry to charitable works. So Vincent worked to assist or free galley slaves and also to collect money from wealthy patrons to create homes and hospitals for orphans. In 1625, he founded the Congregation of the Missions ("Vincentians" or "Lazarists"), a society of priests devoted to rural missionary work and training priests. In 1633, he and St. Louise de Marillac co-founded the Sisters (or Daughters) of Charity, who cared for the sick and poor outside of the convent—a policy that was unprecedented.

As his reputation for charity grew, rulers of nations asked Vincent to organize relief efforts in war-torn areas. He also opposed the Jansenist* heresy in France. Vincent died peacefully in 1660 and was canonized in 1737, the patron of charitable societies. (Feast, September 27.)

de Porres, St. Martin (1579–1639)
When Martin was born in Lima, Peru, his father, a Spanish knight, left his mother to raise young Martin alone. After being apprenticed to a barber-surgeon, Martin joined the Dominicans as a lay brother. He cared for the sick and the poor, both those in the priory and those outside, with such care that he became known as "Martin the Charitable."

Like St. Francis of Assisi,* he had a special love for animals and all of God's creatures, and yet his focus was always on serving the poorest and most oppressed, such as the African slaves in Lima. Martin also was a contemplative, spending long hours of prayer before the Blessed Sacrament and receiving Holy Communion frequently. His work was supported by his friends St. Rose of Lima* and St. John Massias. He was canonized in 1962. (Feast, November 3.)

de Sales, St. Francis (1567–1622)
Francis de Sales became one of the greatest leaders of the Catholic Reformation and is known for his spirituality suited for the common person. A gifted student at Paris and Padua, de Sales turned down a promising secular

career and was ordained a priest in 1593. He was appointed to Geneva, the stronghold of Calvinism, where he brought many Calvinists to the Catholic faith through his wisdom, charity, and conciliatory spirit.

De Sales was named bishop of Geneva in 1602 but administered his diocese from Annecy, near Paris. In 1604, he met St. Jeanne François de Chantal,* a widowed laywoman, and became her spiritual director. He helped her to found the Congregation of the Visitation (a women's religious community) at Annecy in 1610.

De Sales was widely known for his popular spiritual and devotional writings, including *Introduction to the Devout Life* (1609) and *Treatise on the Love of God* (1616). For this work, he was declared the patron of the Catholic press and Catholic writers (by Pope Pius XI* in 1923) and a Doctor of the Church (by Pope Leo XIII* in 1887). (Feast, January 24.)

Descartes, René (1596–1650)

Descartes was a Jesuit-educated philosopher who developed a new philosophical system based on mathematics and a quest for the discovery of certain truth. To find this certainty he applied the principle of "methodic doubt." His famous proof for his own existence was *Cogito ergo sum* ("I am thinking,

therefore I exist"). He claimed that God's existence was also demonstrable, because the "idea" of God could not exceed the reality of God.

Although Descartes desired to remain loyal to the Catholic Church, his thought was often novel and extreme (such as his theory that the mind was a purely immaterial reality, totally distinct from the body). So his writings were placed on the Index of Forbidden Books. While he spent most of his life in the Netherlands, he died in Stockholm, Sweden, in 1650, where he was serving as a tutor to Queen Christina.

The Didache (The Teaching of the Twelve Apostles)

This influential Christian writing is divided topically into two parts. The first half, written in the early second century, contrasts the Christian way of life (the "way of light") with the worldly "way of darkness." This gives us insight into the clear moral teachings of the early Church, such as "Do not murder a child by abortion or kill a newborn infant" (*Didache* 2,2).

The second part of the text reflects the Church order of the latter half of the first century. It provides primitive baptismal formulas and prayers for the Eucharist, as well as instructions for distinguishing between true and false apostles* and prophets. This part of the *Didache* is fascinating in that it apparently was composed in a transitional period between the "charismatic" hierarchy of apostles* and prophets of St. Paul's earlier letters, and the later period when the Church was led by bishops and deacons, as described in the Pastoral Epistles.

It also provides a glimpse of the celebration of baptism and the Eucharist in the first century, before set forms and rubrics were developed. For example, "prophets" presiding at a liturgy are invited to pray at certain points as they are led by the Spirit. Although not actually written by an apostle,* this writing was highly regarded and even considered for inclusion in the New Testament canon.

Diocletian (245–313)

The last great persecution against Christianity in the ancient Roman empire was begun in 303 by the emperor Diocletian (ruled 284–305), probably at the instigation of his Caesar, Galerius, who continued the persecution in the East until his death in 311. At first, Diocletian ordered churches demolished and forced the clergy to hand over sacred books and vessels to the authorities. Those who did were termed *traditores* ("those who hand over," the term from which we get the English word "traitor"). The issue of the terms of their reconciliation with the church gave rise to the Donatist* schism.

Later, Diocletian issued a second edict ordering the imprisonment of the clergy, and then a third calling them to offer sacrifice to the Roman gods or face either death or the living death of imprisonment in the mines. The persecution grew and raged unchecked, with thousands of victims reported, including many well-known martyrs: St. Sebastian, a soldier often portrayed pierced with arrows; St. Tarcisius, the boy-saint who died protecting the Eucharist; SS. Cosmas and Damian, Christian physicians; SS. Lucy and Agnes, noblewomen martyrs; SS. Felix, Vincent, Adauctus, Peter of Alexandria, Marcellinus, and many others.

The Church historian Eusebius* reports that in Diocletian's persecution a whole town of Christians in Phrygia was burned to the ground along with everyone in it. This final great "storm" of persecution ended with Galerius' issuing of a rescript on his deathbed and pleading for Christians to pray for his welfare and that of the empire. Constantine* stated at the Council of Nicea* that if as many people of the invading tribes had been slain as Christians were during the Diocletian persecution, there would not be enough of them left to threaten the empire.

Diodore of Tarsus (d. c. 390)

Diodore was an ascetic and philosopher who is often called the father of the Antiochene "school" (or tradition) of Christology. He was the teacher of both St. John Chrysostom* and Theodore of Mopsuestia* near Antioch before he was named bishop of Tarsus in 378. He was also a strong opponent of the emperor Julian's "pagan revival" and of the heresies of Apollinaris* and Arius.*

Diodore was a leading figure at the First Council of Constantinople* in 381. St. Cyril of Alexandria* was concerned that Diodore's theology of Christ could be interpreted in a way that denied Christ's full divinity, as was the case in the thought of Nestorius.*

Diognetus, Letter to

This book is one of the most elegant of the early Christian apologies and is inspiring reading even today. Writing in the mid-to-late second century, the unknown author systematically exposes the foolishness of Greek idolatry and Jewish "superstition." The climax of the work is its portrayal of the nobility of the Christian way of life, as practiced in the Church communities of the time.

Christians are not unusual in their dress or customs, the writer insists, but they stand out in their standards of morality, virtue, and love. Christians are the "soul" or spiritual life force that invisibly holds the world together— and yet the world hates and persecutes them, just as it did the Savior. Appended to this work is a homily, also of unknown authorship.

Dionysius the Areopagite (fifth or sixth century)

This mysterious Greek writer (also called Pseudo-Dionysius) attributed his works to the figure Dionysius in Acts 17:34, who was converted by St. Paul. His writings had tremendous influence on medieval mystics and theologians of both East and West. These works (*The Divine Names, The Celestial Hierarchy, The Ecclesiastical Hierarchy, Mystical Theology*) were heavily influenced by the thought of the Hellenistic Jewish thinker Plotinus (d. 270) and the fifth-century bishop of Alexandria Proclus. The author's emphasis is on the mystical ascent of the soul to God through prayer, contemplation, and the intercession of the saints.

Dioscorus (d. 454)

Dioscorus was the unworthy episcopal successor of St. Cyril of Alexandria* in 444. He used his political influence to support the heretical monk Eutyches* and to depose the patriarch (archbishop) of Constantinople, Flavian, at the "Robber Council" of Ephesus called by the emperor Theodosius II in 449. He and Eutyches taught that Jesus Christ was "out of two natures," but that after their union Christ possessed only the divine nature (the heresy called Monophysitism).

It is unclear whether Dioscorus really misunderstood the true teaching of St. Cyril* and the Alexandrine school; some claim that he was seeking primarily to undermine the influence of the see of Constantinople by condemning its bishop, Flavian. In either case, the Council of Chalcedon* in 451 turned the tables and deposed, excommunicated, and exiled Dioscorus. He is considered a martyr by the Monophysite churches.

Döllinger, Johann (1799–1890)
A prolific Bavarian church historian, Döllinger was a major critic of the papacy of Pope Pius IX,* especially his promulgation of the dogma of the Immaculate Conception and issuing of the *Syllabus of Errors*. He publicly criticized and ultimately rejected the First Vatican Council's definition of papal infallibility and primacy. These criticisms were expressed in his *Letters of Quirinus*.

Döllinger was excommunicated by his bishop in 1871 for these activities and was never reconciled to the Catholic Church. He became a supporter (though not a member) of the "Old Catholic" churches that also rejected certain Catholic doctrines. He produced many scholarly works on the papacy, the Reformation, and other topics in Church history.

Dominic, St. (c. 1170–1221)
Born of a noble Spanish family, Dominic became a cathedral canon at Osma and subprior in 1201. While traveling with his bishop, Diego, in 1203, Dominic first encountered the Albigensian* heresy. The passion grew in Dominic to convert these people through the witness of a poor and simple gospel life. His wish was fulfilled when the pope commissioned Bishop Diego to lead a preaching mission to the Albigensians in Languedoc.

Dominic in principle opposed the crusade* against the heretics, and crusades in general, with the motto: "Logic and persuasion, not force." Because of his effectiveness as a preacher, he was appointed to lead a new mission base at Toulouse, where he gathered a community of preachers. The bishop of Toulouse approved this new "Order of Preachers," but papal approval was delayed because of a moratorium on new religious rules.

Undaunted, Dominic adopted the Rule of St. Augustine,* and so his order was fully approved by Pope Honorius III in 1218. In the next three years before his early death (at age fifty-one), Dominic traveled extensively, preaching and planting his new order. He oversaw the first general chapter in 1220, where the first constitutions were completed.

He died on a missionary journey to Hungary the next year, but by that time there were Dominicans in Italy, France, England, Spain, Scandinavia, Poland, and the Holy Land. Dominic's zeal for the gospel, his poverty and simplicity of life, his friendliness and charity, his love of learning as a tool for evangelization, and his devotion to Mary (through the rosary) all were traits that he instilled in the order that bears his name. His friend, Cardinal Ugolino, became Pope Gregory IX* and canonized Dominic in 1234.

It is said that while his great contemporary St. Francis of Assisi* loved gospel poverty for its own sake (he called it "Lady Poverty"), Dominic saw poverty as a means to be a credible witness to the gospel. He insisted: "The heretics are to be converted by an example of humility and other virtues far more readily than by any external display or verbal battles.... So let us arm ourselves with devout prayers and set off showing signs of genuine humility and barefooted to combat Goliath." (Feast, August 8.)

Donatism

The Donatist schism swept North Africa in the wake of the Diocletian* persecution in the early fourth century. The Donatists, claiming to be the church of the "pure," would not recognize the validity of the ministry of any clergy who had turned over sacred books or vessels to Roman authorities during the Diocletian persecution. They insisted that any clergy who had done so—the so-called *traditores*—could not be forgiven by the Church nor reinstated to ministry. The position of the Catholics, however, was that such forgiveness and recognition of the ministry of reconciled *traditores* could and ought to be extended by the Church.

The schism began when a group of North African bishops from Numidia said that one of the bishops who had consecrated the new bishop of Carthage, Caecilian, in 311 had been a *traditore*, making the consecration invalid. They elected their own bishop of Carthage, Majorinus, who was succeeded by Donatus, from whom the schismatic movement received its name. Though condemned by a number of synods and by the pope, the movement persisted even after Constantine* attempted to suppress it by military action.

Only after St. Augustine* and others persistently exposed the error of the movement did it begin to decline. The Donatist community, along with the Catholics, fell victim to the invasion of North Africa by foreign tribes in the early fifth century.

Duns Scotus, Blessed John (c. 1265–1308)

Known as the "Subtle Doctor" because of the complexity of his thought, this Scot (hence "Scotus") joined the Franciscans around 1280 and studied at Oxford and later in Paris. He eventually taught theology at Oxford, Paris, and Cologne, and was well known for his commentaries on the *Sentences* of Peter* Lombard. However, the originality of his thought (for example, his acceptance of many propositions of Aristotle, and his focus on the primacy of the will over the intellect in guiding human action) made him both controversial in his time and important in the future of Christian thought up to the present.

Scotus' followers, known as the "Scotists," often were at odds with the disciples of St. Thomas Aquinas*

("Thomists"). For example, Scotus believed, differing from Thomas, that Christ would have become incarnate even if mankind had not sinned, so he could reveal the fullness of human existence. He also was the first major theologian to proclaim the doctrine of Mary's immaculate conception. He was beatified by Pope John Paul II* in 1993.

Dupanloup, Felix (1802–78)

As a French Catholic priest, ordained in 1825, Dupanloup was a noted educator who developed a method called the "Catechism of St. Sulpice." After directing a junior seminary for some years, he was consecrated bishop of Orléans, France, in 1849. His mission was to provide freedom of education, which was part of the liberal agenda to free church schools from state control. His efforts succeeded in 1850.

In 1864 he offered an interpretation of Pope Pius IX's* *Syllabus of Errors* that left some room for some conciliation with the modern world. However, Pius IX's strong stands may have influenced Bishop Dupanloup to argue against defining papal infallibility at Vatican I, though he supported the council's teaching on infallibility after it passed.

Eckhart, "Meister" (c. 1260–1328)
Eckhart was a German Dominican theologian and preacher who rose to prominence in the early fourteenth century and was called "Meister" ("master") on account of his excellence in preaching and teaching. However, his teaching was so original that he was accused of heresy, and he died in 1328 while defending his teaching. Pope John XXII condemned twenty-eight propositions in his writings, but refused to declare Eckhart himself a heretic because of his stated intention to be subject to the Church.

Many of Eckhart's teachings were mystical—that is, characterized by the quest to "break through" complexity in order to arrive at the simple "ground" of reality (God), to have the soul "give birth" to the Word of God who has come to dwell there. Eckhart's thought influenced other later medieval mystics (Suso,* Tauler,* Nicholas of Cusa*) as well as later thinkers such as Martin Luther,* Jakob Böhme, and Georg Hegel.

**Elizabeth of Hungary
(or Thuringia), St. (1207–31)**
This charitable woman was the daughter of Andrew II, king of Hungary. She was married to Louis IV of Thuringia (Germany) and constantly served the poor. When he objected that her generosity was too expensive, he witnessed a basket of roses being changed into a basket of bread and was converted. Henceforth, he assisted her in her charity and accompanied her in prayer.

After Louis' death in 1227, Elizabeth was forced to flee to her uncle, a bishop, and joined the Third Order of St. Francis* in Marburg. Her spiritual director, Conrad, was harsh, but Elizabeth grew in sanctity through her submission, until she was removed from his supervision. She continued her work of feeding and caring for the poor until her early death in 1231, at age twenty-four. She was canonized by Pope Gregory IX* four years later (1235). (Feast, November 19.)

Ephrem the Syrian, St. (c. 306–73)
St. Ephrem, known as "the harp of the Holy Spirit," was a contemporary of St. Athanasius* and the Cappadocian fathers. He is significant because his language (Syriac) and worldview (Asian/African, not Greek) were different from these other great fourth-century theologians, yet his insights into the mysteries of faith were equally

profound. However, the uniqueness of Ephrem's theology lay in its expression in the form of poetry rather than a rationally organized, "systematic" form.

Ephrem reflects on the contrasts between Creator and creation, things hidden and things revealed, sacred and historical time, the One (God) and the many. He also approaches in his poetry the Christian themes of faith, salvation, free will, the importance of the body, and others.

As to Ephrem's life, all we know is that he lived in Nisibis—a far outpost of the eastern Roman empire, where he served as a deacon and catechetical teacher. In 363 the city was evacuated, and Ephrem spent the last ten years of his life in ancient Edessa, where he assisted in organizing relief for the poor during a famine. Only then was he exposed to the theological controversies among the Greek-speaking theologians of the East. His teaching in Syriac amazingly complements and confirms the Greek fathers' beliefs. (Feast, June 9.)

Erasmus of Rotterdam, Desiderius (c. 1469–1536)

Erasmus stands out as the greatest international humanist Catholic scholar of the early sixteenth century. "Christian humanism" emerged from the Renaissance as a movement promoting study of the great classics of Greece, Rome, and Christian antiquity (Scripture and the fathers of the Church). Erasmus epitomized this "Christian humanism."

Schooled in the practical spirituality of the Brethren of the Common Life* at Deventer, Erasmus joined the Augustinian canons and was ordained a priest in 1492. He studied successively in Paris, Oxford, Louvain, Turin, and Bologna. While in England, the humanist scholar John Colet urged Erasmus to study Scripture, which led him to pursue intensively the study of Greek.

His first noted work was a collection of Greek and Latin proverbs (1500). This book was followed by the *Handbook of the Christian Soldier* (1504)—showing the importance of scholarship and study for the Christian life—and a satire, *The Praise of Folly* (1509), which he wrote while visiting (St.) Thomas More* and Bishop (St.) John Fisher* in England. His major scholarly works were a new Greek edition of the New Testament, reliable editions of many of the Latin Fathers, and a Latin translation of Origen.*

Erasmus is said to have precipitated (or at least anticipated) the Protestant Reformation by his rejection of scholastic theology and his biting satires of the excesses of devotion and abuses within the Catholic Church. His proposed remedies were to put charity above devotions and to promote the knowledge of the Scripture and of the fathers of the Church. However, because he did not translate these writings into the vernacular, his works were only accessible to scholars or other well-educated readers.

After Martin Luther* came on the scene, Erasmus contested Luther's rejection of human freedom but was suspected by many Catholics of being a crypto-Lutheran because of his earlier satires on Catholic abuses. Erasmus drew close to the Church and continued to plead for peace among the nations becoming embroiled in religious wars. Nonetheless, a number of Erasmus' works were censured by the University of Paris between 1525 and 1542.

After Erasmus' death in 1536, Pope Paul IV also condemned some of his writings, which later became a blanket censure of all his works by Pope Sixtus V in 1590. Today, Erasmus is respected for his dedication to scholarship and his loyalty to the Catholic Church amidst the turmoil of the early Protestant reform.

Escrivá, St. Josemaría (1902–75)

Escrivá founded the influential Catholic organization Opus Dei in Madrid, Spain, in 1928. The focus of this group is the attainment of holiness for all Christians regardless of their state in life. Opus Dei is now a personal prelature of the pope, with its head directly under the pope's authority, while local chapters are under the jurisdiction of the local bishop. Escrivá's most widely read work is a guide to the spiritual life, *The Way*. He was canonized by Pope John Paul II* in 2002. (Feast, June 26.)

Eusebius of Caesarea (260–340)

Eusebius grew up in Caesarea on the coast of Palestine and studied under Pamphilus, whose great library helped him develop as a scholar. Pamphilus' martyrdom in 309 made a lasting impression on Eusebius, who continued to witness to the faith. He was consecrated bishop of Caesarea in 314.

Eusebius is best known for his important though biased biography of the emperor Constantine* and for his history of the Church from Christ to Constantine. That emperor asked him to give the opening address at the Council of Nicea* in 325. In his writings Eusebius quotes or refers to many works that have been lost.

As the Arian* crisis developed, Eusebius sided with the moderate bishops who were uncomfortable with the teaching of Arius but thought that the Council of Nicea's* term *homoousios* ("of the same substance") was too strong to describe the relationship of God the Father and God the Son. Hence he favored the compromise expression that the Son is *homoiousios* ("of like substance") with the Father.

Eusebius' historical writings have given him a lasting place in Christian history. He witnessed the last great persecution of the Christian faith during the Roman era and the emergence of the new Christian era under Constantine, his friend and patron.

Eutyches (c. 378–454)

The head of an important monastery in Constantinople in the fifth century, Eutyches is known as the "Father of Monophysitism." This heresy teaches that before the union of the divine and human natures (that is, before the Incarnation), Christ possessed two natures, but after their union, he possessed only one nature, the divine. Eutyches' doctrine, after being temporarily affirmed by the "Robber Council" of Ephesus in 449, was shortly thereafter condemned by the Council of Chalcedon* in 451. Eutyches apparently died shortly after this council.

Evagrius Ponticus (345–99)

Evagrius was ordained a lector by St. Basil the Great* and a deacon by St. Gregory Nazianzus.* He attended the Second Council of Constantinople* (553) and so impressed the bishop of that city, Nectarius, that he was invited to stay as a teacher to refute heretics. But while in Constantinople he fell into worldliness and, convicted by a dream, fled to Jerusalem to do penance.

From there he went to the Egyptian desert, where he became the abbot of a group of austere monks who followed the spirituality of Origen.* In the desert, he overcame the weaknesses of the flesh that had pursued him and became known for his great holiness and understanding, which are reflected in his writings on prayer and the ascetic life. He died peacefully in 399, just before Bishop Theophilus of Alexandria launched a bitter attack against Evagrius' community for following the "heresies" of Origen. His writings contributed to the development of ascetic life and spirituality, especially in the East.

Fátima, Our Lady of

The Catholic Church has affirmed that the Blessed Virgin Mary appeared six times to three children in a field (Cova da Iria) near Fátima, Portugal, between May 13 and October 13, 1917. The children conveyed Mary's messages, which emphasized praying the rosary, doing penance, and praying for the conversion of Russia. Mary promised that if her message were heeded, Russia and many souls would be converted, a great war would be averted, and peace would come to the world. If her message were neglected, Russia would spread her errors, with terrible results.

She also revealed three "secrets" to the children, the last of which was known only to the pope until it was revealed publicly in 2000. In her last general apparition (she also appeared a seventh time, privately, to one of the original visionaries, Lucia dos Santos, in 1921), Mary revealed her title "Our Lady of the Rosary." At that time, fifty to seventy thousand people witnessed a sign: the sun spinning or dancing in the sky at noonday.

The Catholic Church recognized the apparition as authentic in 1930, and devotion to Mary under the title of "Our Lady of the Rosary" was approved, along with the offering of Holy Communion in reparation for sin on the first Saturday of each month. A consecration of the world to the Immaculate Heart of Mary was made by Pope Pius XII* in 1942, and Russia was similarly consecrated by Pope John Paul II* in 1984.

Fawkes, Guy (1570–1606)

A conspirator in the infamous "Gunpowder Plot," aimed at blowing up the British House of Parliament to promote a Catholic takeover, Guy Fawkes was caught, tortured (to reveal the names of his co-conspirators), and executed in 1606. For centuries thereafter, "Guy Fawkes Day" (November 5) was annually observed in England with public anti-Catholic rallies and persecution of Catholics.

Fénelon, François (1651–1715)

Ordained in 1675, this French priest gained a reputation as an innovative educator (eventually tutoring the grandson of King Louis XIV) and an effective Catholic apologist who helped many Protestants (mainly Calvinist Huguenots) return to the Catholic Church. He became a controversial figure when he began to advocate the Quietist* spirituality of Madame Jeanne Marie Guyon.* Fénelon signed the decrees of the Council of Issy (1695) that condemned Quietism and was made bishop of Cambrai that same year.

However, when Fénelon wrote a defense of interior prayer in his *Explanation of the Sayings of the Saints on the Interior Life* (1697), he was accused of heresy by the prominent Bishop Jacques Bossuet.* This led to a condemnation of a number of propositions of Fénelon's book by Pope Innocent XII in 1699. Fénelon, to his credit, submitted fully to the Church's decision, and spoke out strongly against Jansenism.* He also wrote an influential apologetical work, *Treatise on the Existence of God.*

Finan, St. (d. 661)

The successor of St. Aidan* as bishop of Lindsfarne, an island near England, Finan continued to spread the gospel and Celtic Christian practice in the English province of Northumbria, with the help of its king, Oswin. Some of these Celtic customs and practices, which differed from the English Benedictine tradition, were challenged at the Synod of Whitby.* (Feast, February 17.)

Fisher, St. John (1469–1535)

A leading scholar of his age, Fisher achieved the climax of his career in his appointment as bishop of Rochester (England) and as chancellor of Cambridge University in 1504. He persuaded the famous humanist Erasmus* to teach Greek at Cambridge. A model bishop, he was both an excellent preacher (giving the eulogy at King Henry VII's funeral) and an influential writer, defending the Catholic faith in treatises against Martin Luther* (1523) and Oecolampadius (1527). These writings contributed to the decrees of the Council of Trent.*

Nevertheless, Fisher's defense of Catherine of Aragon's marriage to Henry VIII* made him an enemy of the king. Fisher sought to protect the liberty of the Church in England and caused the phrase "as far as the law of Christ allows" to be added to the king's claim to supremacy over the Church in 1531. Even so, Fisher eventually was imprisoned and beheaded by Henry for treason in 1535. (Feast, with St. Thomas More,* June 22.)

Francis of Assisi, St. (1181–1226)

Francis spearheaded the Catholic poverty or mendicant movement of the thirteenth century. The increased wealth of Europe had led to laxity in faith. As a youth, Francis himself, son of a well-to-do cloth merchant, enjoyed parties and frivolous living, though he also aspired to be a gallant knight. He set off to battle against a neighboring town, but was captured and imprisoned for a year.

Undaunted, the young man set out again, but this time a vision directed him to return to Assisi. A changed person, Francis told his friends he was betrothed to "Lady Poverty." He dressed in rough clothes and begged food. He even received grace to embrace a leper, which immediately dispelled a lifelong revulsion.

One day, praying at a broken-down chapel, San Damiano, he heard God's voice command him: "Rebuild my Church." Francis set out to repair San Damiano and other churches, but as he attracted followers it became clear that God was using Francis to help restore the whole Catholic Church in its quest for holiness through poverty, simplicity, and submission to its leaders. Indeed, when Francis and his little band of friars minor ("little brothers") visited Rome, they won the recognition of Pope Innocent III* in 1210. The pope reportedly had had a dream in which a little poor man (Francis) came and supported the foundation of a tottering St. John Lateran church, the pope's basilica.

When *Il Poverello* ("the Little Poor Man") returned to Assisi, his order grew rapidly and soon included a women's branch founded by St. Clare* in 1212, the "Poor Clares." Meanwhile, Francis was full of missionary zeal, sending his friars out two-by-two to preach a simple message of repentance. Later, he journeyed with the crusaders and attempted to convert the Muslim sultan with a message of peace.

Francis' "Canticle of the Sun" reveals him as a poet who sees God in all of his creation and thus loves each creature as a reflection of God's goodness. Francis gloried in God's creation and had a special love for Christ's incarnation, which he recalled each year by the erection of a Christmas crib or *crèche* (a practice he originated) beginning in 1223.

Francis experienced intense joy in sharing in Christ's sufferings, but his greatest trials were not the result of his extreme poverty and illnesses. He suffered most through seeing the new leaders of his order, under the direction of their "cardinal-protector," Ugolino (later Pope Gregory IX*), moderate the strict poverty and simplicity of his original rule. Ugolino and Pope Honorius III, who approved the new rule (*Regula Bullata*) in 1223, realized that not all who wished to follow the way of Francis could practice poverty as radically as he did. In addition, a "Third Order" was founded in the 1220s for lay people who wished to live the his ideals while remaining "in the world."

Francis himself, withdrawing from the world to pray on Mount LaVerna, received the stigmata, the marks of Jesus' own suffering, in 1224. Two years later he died at his beloved little church, the *Portiuncula* (St. Mary of the Angels). Francis was canonized less than two years after his death by Pope Gregory IX, and his body was laid to rest in a great basilica erected in his honor at the edge of Assisi. He is one of the most widely loved and admired Catholic saints and is the patron saint of Italy, ecologists, and Catholic action. (Feast, October 4.)

Galilei, Galileo (1564–1642)

An Italian astronomer and mathematician, Galileo became embroiled in the first great controversy over the relationship of modern science and the teachings of the Church. Galileo had concluded through observation that the astronomer Copernicus* had been correct in proposing that the planets of the solar system revolve around the sun, not the earth. Because this contradicted the prevalent teaching (and, seemingly, the Bible), Galileo was ordered to recant his teaching after a trial in 1633 and spent the rest of his life (until 1642) under "house arrest."

In 1741 the Catholic Church reversed her judgment against Galileo, which was confirmed by Pope John Paul II* in 1992, when he endorsed a report of a study commission on the "Galileo affair" that he had appointed in 1981. The report declared the error of Galileo's judges in not correctly apprehending the relationship between Galileo's scientific findings and the teachings of the Scriptures and the Church.

Gall, St. (c. 550–645)

St. Gall was a companion of St. Columban,* who separated from him during their missionary journeys in 612 in Switzerland. He lived there as a hermit and his holiness had great influence. A famous Swiss monastery and a city were named after him. (Feast, October 16.)

Gelasius I, Pope St. (d. 496)

Serving as pope from 492 to 496, Gelasius was the first to be called the "Vicar of Christ." He developed the concept of the two powers or "two swords" of the secular power (sword) of the state and the spiritual power (sword) of the Church, both under Jesus' lordship. (Feast, November 21.)

Gerson, Jean (1363–1429)

This French theologian and chancellor of the University of Paris (1395–97; 1401–15) sought an end to the "Great Schism" within the Western church through the "conciliar theory." This theory held that an ecumenical Council is superior to the pope in emergency situations. Gerson supported the French anti-pope and argued at the Council of Constance* that theologians should be able to vote as well as bishops. He assisted in drawing up the Articles of Constance, the intellectual foundation for Gallicanism.

Less controversial were Gerson's outstanding spiritual writings, which synthesized the best of many great Catholic mystics and theologians.

Gertrude the Great, St. (1256–c. 1302)

St. Gertrude was a Cistercian mystic of the second half of the thirteenth century who was converted to Christ at age twenty-five and pursued a contemplative life. She began to have mystical experiences, including visions of the Sacred Heart of Jesus. She wrote a book of prayers, *Exercita Spiritualia*, and a book on Christian mysticism, *Legatus Divinae Pietatis*. (Feast, November 16.)

Giussani, Luigi (1922–)

This Italian priest founded the Catholic renewal movement *Communione e Liberazione* (*Communion and Liberation*). The movement actually began as an extension of Catholic Action in the 1950s, but in the early 1970s adopted the title "Communion and Liberation" to express their belief, against Marxist liberation movements, that true liberation comes from communion with Christ and with others in him. Fr. Giussani has rooted the movement in the Church, following the pastoral plan of Pope John Paul II* and guided by the theology of Romano Guardini, Henri de Lubac,* and Hans Urs von Balthasar.*

The movement is most active in Italy but has branches throughout the world. Though loosely organized, it includes canonically recognized groups for those adults who make a lifetime commitment to the movement (Fraternity of Communion and Liberation, founded in 1982) and those who live as laypeople committed to celibacy, poverty, and obedience (*Memores Domini*, founded in 1988).

Gnosticism

The greatest internal threats to early Christianity were the heresies that fall under the umbrella title of Gnosticism. Various groups claimed to profess the true Christian religion by virtue of a special knowledge (Greek, *gnosis*) that they had received either from one of Jesus' own apostles or from a close follower. The Gnostics' "dualist" philosophy held that the spiritual realm and the material realm are totally opposed to each other and radically separated. Matter was the handiwork of an evil god (the "Demiurge").

The implications of such teachings were radical. The "God of the Old Testament," who created matter, was an evil god. Jesus, the Savior, could not have become human, but only appeared in human form (the heresy called "Docetism") in order to deliver a secret knowledge that would liberate human beings from the bondage of matter. Thus he would lead them, by ascending through a series of spiritual levels, or *aeons*, into the realm of pure spirit—the *pleroma*, or heaven.

Gnostic teachers such as Marcion (the most influential), Valentinus, Secundus, Basilides, and others formed "churches" based on their Gnostic sacred texts and expurgated versions of the gospels and of St. Paul's writings. These writings revealed a "Christ" who was neither actually born nor really suffered and died. Many early Christian writers refuted the Gnostics and their beliefs, including apostolic fathers* such as St. Ignatius of Antioch* and the later apologists, led by Tertullian* and the great "Gnostic fighter," St. Irenaeus of Lyon.*

Irenaeus appealed to the apostolic tradition and the teaching of the four canonical gospels to refute the so-called secret knowledge of the Gnostics. The Catholic Church's fight against this group expedited the formulation of a list of authorized inspired writings (the "canon" of Scripture), of creeds* that expressed authentic Christian beliefs, and of recognition of the authority of the recognized teachers of the Church, particularly the bishops, to teach and interpret the faith.

Goretti, St. Maria (1890–1902)

This "martyr of purity" was only twelve years old when she was brutally murdered for refusing the seduction of an eighteen-year-old youth, Alessandro Serenelli, in 1902. Maria was always a devout girl, the oldest of five children who often cared for the younger siblings, since her mother was a poor widow. In the attack, she was wounded fourteen times with an ice pick, but her only concern as she remained conscious was for her family.

Before she died, she forgave her attacker. He remained unrepentant until eight years later, when in prison he dreamed of Maria standing before him holding fourteen lilies. Alessandro was converted, and after his release from prison lived with Capuchin Franciscans doing penance. Maria was canonized by Pope Pius XII* in 1950. (Feast, July 6.)

Gratian, John (d. no later than 1159)

Known as the "Father of Canon Law," Gratian organized the various laws and teachings of the Catholic Church into a *Concordance of Discordant Canons*. This later developed into the *Decretals of Gratian* or simply the *Decretals*. Containing almost four thousand sources, the *Decretals* quickly became the source book for all courses in Church law at the major universities, such as those at Bologna, Paris, and Oxford. Eventually Gratian's *Decretals* became the first part of the first official code of canon law for the Catholic Church, the *Corpus Juris Canonici*.

The Great Schism (1378–1417)

This division of allegiance between two, and later three, claimants to the papacy of the Catholic Church lasted almost forty years. It began with the election by a number of cardinals of an "anti-pope" (Clement VII) because they thought Urban VI* (pope 1378–89) had become mentally imbalanced. These cardinals (mainly French) argued that they had elected Urban out of fear of reprisal by the Roman people, who reportedly threatened them if they didn't elect an Italian pope.

The election of Urban was almost certainly canonical, but after his election Urban's tirades against bishops, cardinals, and secular rulers who refused to reform at his command alienated them and precipitated the schism. A solution proposed by Conrad of Gelnhausen (based on the thought of Marsilius of Padua and William of Ockham*) was the summoning of an ecumenical council by the cardinals, even without the consent of the pope. This "conciliar theory" was implemented unsuccessfully at the

Council of Pisa (1409), which only produced a third claimant to the papacy, and successfully at the Council of Constance* (1414–18), which ended the schism with the universal acceptance of the election of Pope Martin V in 1417. The Great Schism weakened the Church and harmed the effectiveness and reputation of the papacy.

Gregory I (the Great), Pope St. (c. 540–604)

Gregory was born of a wealthy, influential Christian Roman family. In his mid-thirties, he abruptly left a prominent position in civil government to become a monk. He founded seven monasteries on family property, six in Sicily and St. Andrew's in Rome, where he resided.

In 579, the pope called Gregory to serve the Church in Rome as a deacon and soon sent Gregory as his personal ambassador to Constantinople to procure military help. In 586, Gregory was recalled to Rome to help heal a schism. Floods in Rome and an outbreak of the plague in 589 led to the death of Pope Pelagius II, and Gregory was the overwhelming choice as his successor. He was the first monk to be elected pope.

Gregory reluctantly accepted his election, preferring the contemplative life of the monastery. Despite constant ill health due to his strict asceticism, he worked tirelessly in every dimension of papal responsibility, from mundane administration to scholarly work in exegesis and liturgy. Given his health and the tremendous burdens of leadership, it is not surprising that his most profound biblical writing, the *Moralia*, is on the book of Job. Throughout his papacy he stressed the virtue of humility; his favorite title for himself was "servant of the servants of God."

The Roman Empire at that time was enduring many trials, which Gregory faced with courage. He negotiated a truce with the fierce Lombards. His concern for the safety and physical needs of his people matched his concern for their spiritual welfare. His pastoral writings reflect his view that the spiritual was primary, since the world was fragile and passing.

To the bishops he wrote the book *Pastoral Care,* which imparted wisdom in guiding the faithful through their preaching and in helping them discern their call to the contemplative or active life. He drew especially from the thought of St. Augustine of Hippo* in his pastoral and theological writings. He also wrote the *Dialogues,* presenting the miraculous deeds of the saints, with special attention to St. Benedict.*

The Benedictine monks played a special role in Gregory's plan of evangelization. The humorous story of his encountering a young Angle lad in a slave market (and making the pun that he was not an Angle, but an "angel") is no doubt a legend. But it is true that he sent St. Augustine of Canterbury* and a band of monks to bring the gospel to "Angle-land" (England). The conversion of King Ethelbert at Kent began the Christianization of that country. A wave of monk-missionaries, in full and loving communion with Rome, continued to spread the gospel there and later brought the Catholic faith to every corner of continental Europe.

Gregory's exemplary life as a monk, his courage as a defender of his people (especially the poor), his skill as a diplomat and an administrator, his wisdom as a pastor, and his vision and zeal for the conversion of nations all attest to his right to be remembered as Pope St. Gregory the Great, and to be numbered among the four great Latin doctors of the early Church. (Feast, September 3.)

Gregory II, Pope St. (669–731)

A master diplomat and a fearless defender of the Catholic faith with a passion for missionary expansion, Gregory II (pope 715–31) was the greatest pope of the eighth century. He protected the people of Rome from invasion, keeping peace with the Lombards. He encouraged the missionary work in Germany of Wynfrith, whom he renamed Boniface.* This support assured that the infant church in Germany would adopt the Roman liturgy and have strong ties to the see of Peter through Boniface and his monk-missionaries.

Gregory's contemporary, the Byzantine emperor Leo III (the Isaurian), provoked the iconoclast controversy in the East, which condemned the veneration of sacred images (icons) and sought to destroy them. Leo made threats against Rome, demanding that Gregory support his iconoclasm. But the pope ignored the threats and strenuously condemned iconoclasm as a heresy. (Feast, February 13.)

Gregory III, Pope St. (d. 741)

Gregory III was pope (731–41) at the height of the iconoclast controversy, which had begun in the reign of his immediate predecessor, Gregory II.* Remarkably, Gregory was the last pope to remain loyal to the Byzantine emperor in principle, though he vigorously opposed the emperor's policies of destruction of sacred images. He also supported the missionary work of Boniface in Germany (making him an archbishop) and of the Benedictines* in England, granting their leaders the

pallium, a vestment given to key Church leaders signifying their unity with the pope. (Feast, November 28.)

Gregory VII, Pope St. (c. 1021–85)

One of the great popes of the Middle Ages, Gregory VII gave his name to the "Gregorian Reform" that took place during his reign. It was symbolic of the ascendancy of the papacy that one of the most powerful rulers of Europe (Henry IV) was forced to his knees in repentance after Gregory excommunicated him.

Hildebrand (his family name) studied in Rome and took monastic vows. He served almost thirty years as a delegate and chief advisor of the popes. He helped Pope Nicholas II develop the papal election decree of 1059, which placed the election of popes in the hands of the cardinals.

In 1073, Hildebrand was elected pope by popular acclaim, taking the name Gregory after Pope St. Gregory I (the Great).* His reform measures started in 1074 with a Lenten Synod condemning simony and immoral clergy. In 1075, he attacked lay investiture (rulers' appointing clergy and investing bishops with signs of their spiritual office) and vigorously proclaimed the universal authority of the pope in *Dictatus Papae*.

This claim was put to the test by the

German emperor Henry IV, who denounced Gregory as a "false monk" and declared him deposed. Gregory responded by excommunicating Henry and freeing his subjects from allegiance to him. With his support crumbling, Henry repented on his knees in the snow at the castle of Canossa in January 1077, where the pope was staying.

Gregory forgave him and lifted the excommunication, but when Henry regained power, his troops moved against Rome in 1084. The pope was rescued by Robert Guiscard and the Normans, but the Norman soldiers looted and burned parts of Rome. The angry Romans forced Gregory to flee in 1085 to Salerno, where he died with the last words: "I have loved righteousness and hated iniquity, therefore I die in exile."

Although Gregory's life seemed to end in failure, he succeeded in many of his reform efforts and in restoring the moral and political leadership of the papacy. He also condemned the erroneous Eucharistic teaching of Berengar of Tours (c. 1010–88), who denied that there is a real change in the elements of bread and wine when consecrated at Mass. Gregory was canonized in 1606. (Fcast, May 25.)

Gregory IX, Pope (c. 1148–1241)

A nephew of Pope Innocent IV, Count Ugolino of Segni was well trained in theology, canon law, and Church service. Before his election as pope in 1227, he had served as cardinal-protector of the Franciscan order and preached the Fifth Crusade* (1218–21). As soon as he was elected pope he launched the Sixth Crusade* (1228–29) and excommunicated Emperor Frederick II for apparently refusing to participate.

Later Frederick joined the crusade, but Gregory didn't lift the excommunication until 1230. After an eight-year truce with Frederick, the pope reimposed the excommunication after discovering the emperor's attempt to gain control of Italy. Frederick's forces marched to Rome to capture Gregory, but he died with the troops at Rome's gates.

Gregory was a courageous leader of the Church, a noted advocate of Church renewal, and the pope who approved and promulgated the first complete collection of papal decretals, the *Liber extra,* compiled by Spanish Dominican St. Raymond of Peñafort. This collection served as the primary source of canon law until the twentieth century.

Gregory XI, Pope (1329–78)

A French cardinal, Gregory XI was only forty-two when elected to the papacy in 1370, but his poor health and the rigors of his office led to his death in 1378. He is noted for moving the see of St. Peter back to Rome, after sixty-eight years in Avignon. He had expressed his intention to make this move early in his papacy, but lack of finances and political considerations prevented him from leaving Avignon before 1376.

The move from France was abetted by the prophetic urging of St. Catherine of Siena,* who stayed at Avignon for three months in the summer of 1376. When Gregory finally arrived back in Rome in 1377, he encountered so many problems and so much opposition that he went to Anagni, where he died in the midst of a political struggle with Florence. Nonetheless, he is admired for his courage and perseverance. In spite of being a loyal Frenchman, he put the interests of the Church first in courageously returning the papacy to Rome.

Gregory of Nazianzus, St. (329–89)

Gregory was the Cappadocian father known as "the Theologian." His father was bishop of Nazianzus (northeast of modern Turkey), who sent him to study in Athens, where he met his life-long friend, St. Basil.* He and Basil both returned to Cappadocia and lived as monks.

Like Basil, Gregory was pressed into the service of the Church, being ordained a priest (c. 362) and then consecrated bishop of Nazianzus, succeeding his father. He was summoned to Constantinople in 379, where his powerful preaching for Nicene* orthodoxy prepared the way for the defeat of Arianism* at the First Council of Constantinople* in 381. The council named him bishop of Constantinople, but he served there less than a year because of failing health.

Gregory is known for his theology of the Holy Spirit as a fully divine Person (not just an "energy"), for his poems, for his refutation of the heresies of Apollinarius,* and for the *Philocalia,* a collection of writings of the Eastern fathers which he compiled with St. Basil. (Feast, shared with Basil, January 2.)

Gregory of Nyssa, St. (335–95)

The younger brother of St. Basil the Great* and St. Macrina,* Gregory was the most philosophically astute and mystically profound of the "Cappadocian fathers." With Basil and Gregory of Nazianzus,* he developed the doctrine of the Trinity and especially of the divinity of the Holy Spirit. He was educated through his brother, Basil, and through St. Gregory Thaumaturgos* (who had converted his grandmother St. Macrina the Elder). He was also exposed to the works of Origen,* who greatly influenced his thought.

The Second Council of Nicea* (787) called Gregory of Nyssa "the Father of the Fathers" for his many important writings. These works include treatises against heresies; catechetical writings, such as his *Catechetical Orations;* exegetical works, such as *Life of Moses;* and ascetical works, such as *On Virginity,* in which he speaks of the soul of the virgin as the spouse of Christ. He also wrote a biography of his sister, St. Macrina.

Though a great theologian, Gregory was unsuccessful as a bishop because he lacked administrative skills. He made a significant contribution in overturning Arianism* and the *Pneumatomachi* (or Macedonian) heresy against the divinity of the Holy Spirit. (Feast, March 9.)

Gregory of Tours, St. (c. 540–94)

A native of Gaul, Gregory became the nineteenth bishop of Tours in 537. Though his Latin was not polished, he was one of the most educated men of his time and wrote lives of the saints, a biography of St. Martin of Tours,* and *The History of the Franks* (written 573–91). The second half of this last work recounts the conversion and reign of Clovis,* the "new Constantine,"* whose successful and bloody wars established Catholicism as the sole religion of what was soon to be medieval France. (Feast, November 14.)

Gregory Thaumaturgus, St. (c. 213–70)

We know the life of this saint mainly through a biography written by St. Gregory of Nyssa,* whom he influenced. Born in Pontus (south of the Black Sea), Gregory was taught by Origen* in Caesarea for five years (roughly 233–38) and was converted by him to Christianity. After this, Gregory returned home and was made bishop of Neocaesarea, where he faithfully served throughout the Decian persecution* (250–51) until his death sometime in the reign of Aurelian (270–75).

Gregory is best known today for his sound teaching (St. Gregory of Nyssa called him simply "the Teacher"), such as his principle work, *The Exposition of Faith,* which he said was given to him in a vision by St. John the Evangelist through the intercession of the Blessed Virgin Mary. However, at the time he was better known for the "wonders" (miracles) that Nyssa recounts he performed by faith and prayer—hence his title *Thaumaturgus*, "the Wonder Worker." Though some of the tales of mighty works seem like legends, it is a fact that through Gregory's ministry as bishop, most of the city of Pontus converted to Jesus Christ. (Feast, November 17.)

Groote, Gerhard (1340–84)

Born of a wealthy merchant family in the Netherlands around 1340, Groote had a highly successful academic career. While teaching in Cologne, he left his career in 1374 and spent three years in a Carthusian monastery fostering his spiritual life. After being ordained a deacon, he preached the need for the Church to reform and practice poverty.

Groote attracted many followers who later joined together to form the Brethren of the Common Life,* modeled on a group of sisters that Groote had founded. The popular ascetic movement that he led, which emphasized biblically oriented spirituality, the practice of charity, and community life, was part of a wider renewal movement called the *Devotio Moderna*. Thomas à Kempis,* the movement's most prominent spiritual guide, wrote a biography of Groote, who died of the plague in 1384.

Guyon, Madame (1648–1717)

Madame Guyon (Jeanne Marie Bouvier de la Mothe) became the first French leader of Quietism,* a movement started in Spain by Miguel de Molinos,* whose teaching was condemned by the Church in 1687. Guyon had studied Molinos' teaching at the advice of her spiritual director (Barnabite priest F. Lacombe). Both Guyon and Lacombe were imprisoned for some months because of their teaching about the need for total passivity before God in mystical prayer.

Archbishop François Fénelon* was Madame Guyon's advocate and helped establish her in the French court. However, her teachings were formally condemned by the Council of Issy in 1695. Her theology of complete detachment from the world and total submission to God's will in humility and simplicity was echoed by the German pietists, Quakers, and some English evangelicals in the eighteenth century.

Haraldsson, St. Olaf (995–1030)

Known as the "Eternal King" and patron saint of Norway, Olaf was a violent Viking warrior in his youth. He enlisted to serve the English and was converted to Christianity and baptized at Rouen (in Normandy) in 1013. At age twenty he unified Norway and became king, establishing a code of law (*Kristenret*) that was clearly Christian: It outlawed pagan worship, infanticide, and polygamy. In addition, it authorized the Church to regulate marriages, feast days, and fasts.

Olaf was known for his fairness and mercy, but he also harshly repressed heathen resistance to his rule. After a twelve-year reign, he was expelled by King Knut (Canute) of England and Denmark, and he fled to Russia. When he returned in 1030 to regain his throne (for Christ, he said, not for himself) he was killed in battle. Many miracles were reported during and after the battle, which led to the canonization of this popular missionary-king only eleven years later (1041). (Feast, July 29.)

Helena, St. (c. 250–330)

Helena was the mother of the emperor Constantine.* At her instigation, a number of major basilicas were constructed, including the Holy Sepulchre in Jerusalem and the Church of the Nativity in Bethlehem. What she believed to be the relics of the "true cross" of Christ were unearthed in Jerusalem. Following in Helena's footsteps, many Christians have gone on pilgrimage to the Holy Land. (Feast, August 18.)

Henoticon

The Roman emperor Zeno attempted to unite the followers of the Council of Chalcedon* and the Monophysites with the Christological formula known as the *Henoticon*, written in 482 by Bishop Acacius of Constantinople. The Monophysites were generally pleased with the formula, but since no reference was made to the *Tome* of Pope Leo I,* which was vital to the Chalcedonian definition, the pope rejected the formula and excommunicated Acacius. Thus the formula failed to reconcile the Catholic Church and the Monophysites.

Henry II, St. (972–1024) and Kunigunde, St. (d. 1033)

This saintly married couple worked together for the promotion of the

Church through reform efforts, founding monasteries, and building churches, such as the famous cathedral at Bamberg. They were married in 998. Four years later Henry succeeded Otto II as king of Bavaria and finally was crowned Holy Roman emperor by Pope Benedict VIII in 1014.

Henry's political career was a constant struggle to revive the declining Holy Roman Empire. He was fairly successful in Germany, investing bishops who would support his reform, which included denouncing clerical marriage and incontinence. He and Kunigunde were patrons of the Cluniac* monasteries and friends of the poor. They sought to establish services to help and care for them.

After Henry's death, Kunigunde put off her imperial robes and became a religious, devoting herself to prayer and to care of the sick until her death. Henry, canonized in 1146, was viewed in the Middle Ages as a model Christian king. (Henry's feast, July 13; Kunigunde's, March 3.)

Henry VIII, King (1491–1547)

English king from 1509–47, Henry VIII broke from the Catholic Church because of the refusal of Pope Clement VII to grant him an annulment of his marriage to Catherine of Aragon (a marriage that had been validated by Pope Julius II). Ironically, Henry had been declared a "Defender of the Faith" by Pope Leo X* for his writings against Protestantism and his support of papal authority. But the annulment issue changed Henry's views, and after his chancellor, Cardinal Thomas Wolsey, failed to obtain the annulment in 1529, Henry proceeded to move against the Catholic Church in England.

After five years, Henry declared himself the "supreme head" of the English Church, establishing the "Church of England" or the Anglican Church. He executed the few Catholic leaders who dared to oppose him, notably (St.) Thomas More,* Henry's former friend and chancellor of England, and Bishop (St.) John Fisher* of Rochester.

Apart from the issue of authority, Henry's spirituality remained traditionally Catholic. However, his personal appointee as archbishop of Canterbury was Thomas Cranmer. Cranmer annulled Henry's marriage to Catherine, produced a *Book of Common Prayer* that became the new basis of Anglican worship, and fostered a scriptural spirituality for the Church of England drawn from the continental Reformers. Cranmer's work gave the Anglican church a more distinctively Protestant flavor than the institution foreseen by Henry.

Hermas (second century)

This mysterious figure is counted among the apostolic fathers* because he wrote *The Shepherd*, which was regarded by St. Irenaeus,* St. Clement of Alexandria,* and other Eastern fathers as an inspired book of Scripture. Hermas' identity is shadowy, but *The Shepherd* situates its author as writing from Rome in the mid-second century.

The book begins with a series of visions, culminating in a vision of an "angel of repentance" dressed like a shepherd who reveals twelve "mandates" (of the Christian moral life) and ten parables that employ powerful images to convey Christian principles. This writing was widely read in the Greek-speaking East in the second and third centuries and often was used as a textbook for catechumens.

Hilary of Poitiers, St. (315–68)

A pagan from the Roman province of Gaul, Hilary became such an exemplary Christian that shortly after his conversion he was named bishop of Poitiers in 353. But the Arian* emperor Constantius II had just taken power in the West, so he exiled the staunchly pro-Nicene* Hilary to Phrygia in the East. Here the bishop learned about the monastic movement, and when he returned he helped establish monasticism in the West through St. Martin of Tours.*

Hilary composed one of the first great Latin theological works, *On the Trinity*, to refute Arianism. He also called together a synod at Gaul to oppose this heresy. His courage and wisdom caused him to be declared not only a saint but a Doctor of the Church by Pope Pius IX* in 1851. (Feast, January 13.)

Hildegard of Bingen, St. (1098–1179)

Hildegard was a German mystic and a visionary whose influence affected many in the twelfth century—from emperor Fredrick I Barbarossa and St. Bernard of Clairvaux* to the Benedictine sisters in her convent and the common people who read her prophetic words and sang her hymns. Although she had received visions since age eight, it was not until her early forties that she began to write them down (in the *Scivias*). They were approved by Pope Alexander III and were widely read. These writings focus attention on the need for conversion and a closer following of the Lord. (Feast, September 17.)

Hippolytus, St. (c. 170–c. 236)

Hippolytus bears the distinction of being the first "anti-pope"—someone claiming to be pope in opposition to the rightful holder of the office. He is also the first prominent schismatic to be reconciled to the Catholic Church and later declared a saint. His writings in Greek indicate that he was born in the East, but he became prominent as a priest-theologian in Rome.

Though he attacked the false teaching of Sabellius about the Trinity, two popes accused him of dividing the Father and the Son into two gods ("ditheism"). His most noted writings are his *Refutation of All Heresies* (or *Philosophoumena*, c. 222) and his accounts of early Church order and liturgy in *The Apostolic Tradition* (c. 215). When tensions over his theology grew between Hippolytus and Popes Zephyrinus (198–217) and Callistus* (217–22), Hippolytus finally formed his own church.

In particular, Hippolytus found Pope Callistus too lax in his standards for the reconciliation and readmission of those who fell into serious sin. Like Tertullian,* Hippolytus was a rigorist who demanded a pure, undefiled Church, not Callistus' view of the Church as a "Noah's Ark" bearing both the "clean" and the "unclean." Providentially, both Hippolytus and Pope Pontian(us) (pope 230–35) were exiled to Sardinia, where tradition holds that Hippolytus made his peace with the Church before he and Pontian were martyred. As early as the fourth century, under Pope St. Damasus I,* Hippolytus was honored as a martyr. He and Pope St. Pontian now share the same feast day (August 13).

Hofbauer, St. Clement Mary (1751–1820)

The patron saint of Vienna, Austria, St. Clement became a Redemptorist priest in Rome in 1784 and first did social and religious work in Warsaw among German-speaking Poles. In 1808, he was forced by Napoleon's edicts to leave Poland. He moved to Vienna, where he confronted the harm done by the anti-religious policies of Joseph II* and established a college. Clement was canonized by Pope Pius X* in 1909. (Feast, March 15.)

Honorius I, Pope (d. 638)

Although Honorius I exhibited strong leadership in missionary outreach to the Anglo-Saxons and in reforming the Church in Rome, he is best remembered today for one theological statement. In the struggle of the Eastern Churches with the Monophysite and Monothelite heresies (the latter held that Christ had only one will, the divine), Patriarch Sergius of Constantinople wrote to Honorius for his opinion. In reply, the pope seemed to be accepting Sergius' view that Jesus had only one will (Monothelitism).

When this position was condemned by the Third Council of Constantinople* in 681, Honorius' name was listed among those guilty of this heresy. Pope Leo II approved the council's teaching and admitted that Pope Honorius I had "allowed [the Church's] purity to be sullied," failing to condemn Monotheletism.

This issue has been magnified in importance due to the discussion of papal infallibility in the nineteenth century. Some argued that Honorius' teaching proves that the pope is not infallible; others wrote that Honorius' statement was not put forth as dogma or formal teaching of the Church, but merely as an opinion expressed in a response to Sergius. The Catholic Church has always held that there is no evidence that Pope Honorius was guilty of heresy by actively teaching Monotheletism.

Hopkins, Gerard Manley (1844–89)

A convert to the Catholic Church (1866), and later a Jesuit priest (1877), Hopkins has become one of the most influential modern Catholic poets. Known for rhythmic flowing verse and creative use of words, he also accentuates Christian themes that express adoration of God and glory in his creation.

Humbert of Silva Candida (d. 1061)

Humbert was a learned monk when he was made a cardinal-bishop by Pope Leo IX in 1050. He was known for his zeal for reform, calling for an end to lay investiture and simony. In 1054, Humbert was sent to Constantinople by Leo IX to help clarify some statements of the patriarch of that city that implied disloyalty or disrespect to the pope.

After spending a number of months in Constantinople without an audience, Humbert composed a bill of excommunication of the Eastern Church and laid it on the altar of the patriarch's church (*Hagia Sophia*). Thus the Great Schism* of Eastern and Western Christianity began. Ironically, Humbert may not have been authorized to issue this bill, since (unbeknownst to him) Pope Leo IX had died before the bull of excommunication was issued.

Huss, John (c. 1372–1415)

Huss led a major schismatic movement in Prague, which was a precursor of the Protestant Reformation. Born a peasant, he sought social advancement through priestly training and eventually was ordained in 1400. He was named dean of the Philosophy Faculty at the University of Prague in 1401 and was a popular preacher at Prague's large "Bethlehem Chapel."

Huss was influenced by the biblical interpretation of Englishman John Wycliffe* and was increasingly critical of the Catholic Church, attacking the immorality of the clergy, indulgence selling, and papal authority. Pope Alexander V ordered the burning of Wycliffe's books and the cessation of preaching in private chapels, and the anti-pope John XXIII answered Huss' attack on indulgences by excommunicating him. Huss moved out of Prague and wrote his major treatise on the Church. (The first ten chapters were all from Wycliffe.)

Huss traveled to the Council of Constance* (1414) hoping to vindicate his views. But despite a promise of "safe conduct" from the Emperor Sigismund, he was arrested, tried for heresy, and finally convicted and burned at the stake on July 6, 1415. He immediately became a Czech national hero and inspired rebellion against the emperor and the Catholic Church.

Huss also inspired Martin Luther* and other sixteenth-century Protestant reformers, who agreed with his focus on Scripture as the sole source of authority, his rejection of indulgences and other Catholic practices, and his insistence on the right of national churches to make pastoral decisions and to worship in their own language. The *Unitas Fratrum* (Union of Brethren) and the Moravian brethren trace their origins to Huss' teaching.

Ignatius of Antioch, St. (c. 35–c. 115)

Bishop of one of the most prominent sees of the ancient Church, Ignatius was captured and led to trial in Rome by a band of Roman soldiers (whom he called "ten leopards"). On his journey, he wrote letters to churches along the way, seven of which have been preserved. These letters provide remarkable insights into the pastoral situation of the Church just a generation after the apostles.*

Ignatius speaks of the imperative of unity in the Church, preserved through communion with the hierarchy, comprising a single bishop, presbyters, and deacons in each local church. This leadership structure from the year 110 is the same found today in the Catholic Church. Unity in the one faith is guarded by Ignatius as he refutes the heresies of the "Judaizers" (who denied the divinity of Jesus Christ) and the Docetists (Gnostics* who denied Christ's humanity, seeing him as a pure spirit merely appearing to be human).

Ignatius' most memorable statements, though, center around his desire for martyrdom. He speaks of "living water" beckoning him to "come to the Father," and he pleads with the church in Rome to make no attempt to prevent his martyrdom: "I long to be ground by lion's teeth to become pure bread for Christ.... That is when I will really be a Christian, when the world sees me no more." Ignatius' greatest longing was fulfilled when he was martyred in Rome sometime between 107 and 110. (Feast, October 17.)

Ignatius Loyola, St. (c. 1491–1556)

A Spanish soldier-of-fortune, Ignatius became a soldier for Christ and founded the most influential religious order of the Catholic Reformation: the Society of Jesus (the "Jesuits"). His religious conversion began in 1521. While recovering from a severe leg injury, he read lives of Christ and the saints, which inspired his resolve to become a saint himself. He hung up his sword and dedicated his life to Christ at Monserrat in 1522, and then lived an ascetic life for nearly a year in a cave near Manresa. There he began to compose his *Spiritual Exercises*, which became the basis for the Jesuits' "Ignatian" method of spiritual direction and discernment of spirits.

After a pilgrimage to Jerusalem,

Ignatius discerned the need of education to "help souls," and so for the next eleven years (1524–35) he became a student in Spain and at the University of Paris. In Paris, he recruited six men, including (St.) Francis Xavier* and (Blessed) Peter Faber, to become the nucleus of his "Company of Jesus." After graduating from Paris, Ignatius prepared his company to serve the Church in the Holy Land, but due to political conditions it was impossible to travel there. Instead, they went to Rome, where the first rule of his order was approved by Pope Paul III* in 1540 and named "The Society of Jesus."

This was a new type of religious order. The Divine Office was not chanted or recited in choir; instead, Jesuits were sent out by twos or in small groups either to do missionary work, to teach, or to minister to those in need. They were at the disposal of the pope, and a "fourth vow" of loyalty to him was added for Jesuits who had belonged to the order for some time. Ignatius was elected the first general of the order in 1541 and governed it from Rome until his death. He founded a Roman College (later Gregorian University) and a German college to form his priests. (Feast, July 31.)

Innocent III, Pope (1160–1216)

If one were to seek the apex of papal power over the past two millennia, both in the Church and the world, the pontificate of Innocent III may be that apex. Elected in 1198 at age thirty-seven, Lotario Scotti was a theologian, canon lawyer, and cardinal deacon. He saw himself as the "Vicar (representative) of Christ," who was set above man to govern, not only the universal Church, but the whole world.

In secular affairs, Innocent exerted remarkable power. He reestablished control over the papal states; selected and crowned rulers for Germany; excommunicated King John of England for refusing to recognize Stephen Langton as archbishop of Canterbury, placing England under interdict (no sacraments administered except baptism) until he submitted; and compelled King Philip II of France to return to the wife he had divorced. When the Cathari heretics in France could not be persuaded to repent, he launched the Albigensian* crusade, which greatly weakened them.

Innocent's greatest failure on the world scene was the ill-fated Fourth Crusade,* in which the crusaders sacked Constantinople (1204) and set up a Latin kingdom. This disastrous venture rendered the schism between Eastern and Western Christianity practically irreparable for centuries. To his credit, Innocent III had nothing to do with the crusaders' agenda. But he accepted the outcome afterwards as a *fait accompli* and approved the establishment of a Latin patriarchate in Constantinople, mistakenly thinking this would eventually promote reunion of the divided churches.

Innocent's leadership and foresight are shown more clearly in his endeavors within the Church. He was a reforming pope who reduced the luxury of the papal court and promoted honesty in the curia (church administration). He sought to involve bishops more actively in decision making and called the greatest reform council in the Middle Ages, the Fourth Lateran Council.* Best of all, he approved and encouraged the new mendicant orders of St. Francis* and St. Dominic* and reconciled many schismatic and heretical groups to the Church. Pope Innocent III was a great pope who established the thirteenth century as the "height of Christendom."

Inquisition

This term refers to a legal inquiry into possible heretical teaching that threatens the truth and integrity of Catholic faith. The first form of the Inquisition, established by Pope Lucius III in 1184, was directed by the bishops.

When this proved ineffective against the Cathari heretics, Pope Gregory IX* (1233) called for a papal Inquisition, conducted by the newly established Dominican* and Franciscan* orders.

The goal of the process was conversion, though an individual found guilty of heresy was punished by the secular authorities, since heresy was considered a serious crime threatening the existence of the Christian state. For those who confessed guilt quickly and voluntarily, the penalty might be a pilgrimage to Jerusalem or confiscation of property. Recalcitrant convicted heretics were burned at the stake.

A limited use of torture in the inquisitorial process was allowed by Pope Innocent IV (in *Ad extirpanda*), but there is no evidence that this was widely practiced in the thirteenth century. After the Albigensian* heresy was rooted out by the end of the thirteenth century, the Inquisition was suspended, until revitalized in Spain in the late fifteenth century.

Irenaeus, St. (c. 125–c. 202)

Irenaeus is well named, for this irenic man brought peace to the Church in a number of situations, especially to second-century Christians troubled by the Gnostic* heresy. Born in Asia Minor, in his youth Irenaeus sat at the feet of St. Polycarp of Smyrna,* who

had been discipled by the apostle*
John. Hence, Irenaeus had firsthand
experience of "apostolic tradition" and
"apostolic succession"—how the
Church's faith was handed on through
the succession of bishops going back
to the apostles.

On becoming a priest, Irenaeus was
sent to Lyons in the Roman province
of Gaul. In 177 he brought a letter to
Pope Eleutherius seeking tolerance for
the Montanist* movement. While
Irenaeus was in Rome, Pothinus, the
bishop of Lyons, was martyred;
Irenaeus became Lyon's second bishop.

As bishop, he fought the insidious
Gnostic heresy, which denied Christ's
true humanity. His five-volume work
Against Heresies stressed the full
humanity of the incarnate Jesus, showing how this was the teaching of the
apostles* and the unbroken tradition
of the Catholic Church. He is also
known for his doctrine of "recapitula-
tion"—that all creation is "summed
up" and finds its completion in Jesus
Christ. Irenaeus' teaching turned the
tide against the Gnostics and won him
acclaim as the Church's first systematic
theologian. His only other preserved
work, aside from a few fragments, is a
brief, later writing, the *Demonstration
of the Apostolic Tradition*.

Always a peacemaker, Irenaeus
convinced Pope Victor II to lift his

excommunication of some Christians
in Asia Minor (the Quartodecimans)
who celebrated Easter on a different
day from the rest of the Church.
(Feast, June 28.)

Jansen, Cornelius (1585–1638)

Jansen was a Dutch theologian who was made director of the University of Louvain in 1617, shortly after its founding, and was consecrated as bishop of Ypres in 1636. He collaborated with the French Abbé de St.-Cyran to develop a theology of grace based on St. Augustine's* writings. This theology was summarized in Jansen's book, *Augustinus*, which was published two years after his death, in 1640.

Jansen's thought gave rise to the Jansenist movement. St.-Cyran caused his ideas to be accepted at the convent of Port-Royal near Paris. After St.-Cyran's death in 1643, the movement was led by Antoine Arnauld and supported by the great French mathematician Blaise Pascal.*

The Jansenists claimed to be teaching what St. Augustine* taught about grace and free will, but actually their theology was a Calvinist* interpretation of Augustine. With Calvinism, Jansenism holds that Christ did not die for all (therefore only some people are predestined to be saved), that the grace of God is irresistible, and that the sign of God's election is the ability to live a very strict, austere moral life. This austerity, which often manifested itself in scrupulosity, was prevalent at Port-Royal and elsewhere among Jansen's followers.

The greatest enemies of the Jansenists in France were the Jesuits, whom they accused of moral laxity, especially in spiritual direction and confessional practices. Pascal's *Provincial Letters* contain a trenchant and critical attack on the Jesuits' theology of grace and confessional practices.

Some major propositions of Jansenism were first condemned by Pope Innocent X in the bull *Cum Occasione* (1653). The Jansenists claimed that those tenets did not reflect their doctrine fairly. Clement IX (pope 1667–69) allowed the Jansenists to hold their beliefs privately, with "respectful silence."

However, Pasquier Quesnel's book, *Moral Reflections*, reaffirmed Jansenist propositions publicly, and the movement was finally condemned by a bull of Pope Clement XI, *Unigenitus*, in 1713. This action was supported by the French King Louis XIV, who suppressed the convent of Port-Royal and persecuted the Jansenists, many of whom fled to the Netherlands and other countries. Although Jansenism as an organized movement has faded from history, the tendency of Jansenism to foster an over-strict morality based on external observations and a fear of not being one of the elect still recurs among Catholics.

Jerome, St. (c. 342–420)

One of the most controversial and colorful of saints, Jerome was also one of the greatest scholars in Church history. Born in Strido, he went to Rome to study the Greek and Roman classics, and there was baptized and pursued the ascetic life. Years later, he had a dream in which the Lord accused him: "You are a Ciceronian, not a Christian." Thereafter Jerome pursued Christian studies exclusively.

He became a hermit in the Syrian desert near Chalcis for four or five years, and there learned Hebrew. In 379 he was ordained a priest in Antioch and attended the First Council of Constantinople.* Jerome then went to Rome with Pope Damasus I,* who commissioned him to produce a new translation of the Bible from the original languages into Latin. This monumental project lasted fifteen years and resulted in the Latin Vulgate edition that was to be the authorized Catholic Bible for over a thousand years.

Jerome was spiritual director for some wealthy women in Rome, but controversy arose over his advice, so he returned to the East. After a pilgrimage he settled in Bethlehem in 386, where he spent the last thirty years of his life in study, writing, and prayer. His cell is preserved in the Church of the Nativity in Bethlehem.

In those years Jerome not only completed the Bible translation but also authored biblical commentaries, numerous essays, and letters against heresies. He was a feared polemicist due to his unassailable scholarship and scorn of heretics. Any enemy of the Church was his enemy, so he refuted Helvidius (who denied Mary's perpetual virginity), Jovinian, Arius,* Pelagius,* and even Origen,* whom he had once admired until the latter's orthodoxy was called into question. Jerome is one of the four great Latin Doctors of the early Church and is often depicted with a quill in hand and a lion at his feet. (Feast, September 30.)

Joachim of Fiore (c. 1132–1202)

Joachim was a mystic of the thirteenth century who is best known for his division of history into three successive ages: the age of the Father (related to the married state), which corresponded to the Old Testament period ruled by the law of Moses; the age of the Son (related to the clergy), which would last forty-two generations of about thirty years each (that is, until about 1260); and the age of the Holy Spirit (related to monks or contemplatives), which would give rise, through the Holy Spirit, to new religious orders that would convert the world and begin a new "spiritual church" (or "church of the Spirit"). Many people were influenced by this prediction, especially groups of "spiritual Franciscans" or "Fraticelli," who saw their adherence to the "primitive observance" of St. Francis'* rule as the fulfillment of Joachim's prophecy of the beginning of the "third age" of the Holy Spirit.

Before he died, Joachim himself submitted judgment of the orthodoxy of his works to the Church's Magisterium. The Fourth Lateran Council* (1215) and the Council of Arles (1263) condemned some sections and interpretations of his writings, but Joachim's memory was still widely respected after his death, and Dante, writing in *The Divine Comedy*, placed him in paradise.

Joan of Arc, St. (1412–31)

Called "the Maid of Orléans," Joan was a French peasant girl who, at the age of thirteen, began to receive supernatural visitations by angels (such as St. Michael) and saints (St. Catherine of Alexandria, St. Margaret) who told her that she was to save France from the English. She persisted in her attempts to meet the heir to the French throne, Charles VII. Finally, Joan identified the disguised Charles in a roomful of courtiers and then revealed to him a secret only known to him.

His theologians confirmed that her inspiration was not demonic. And so at age seventeen, clad in white armor and bearing a banner with the names of Jesus and Mary, she rallied the French army to lift the English siege of Orléans. Shortly thereafter, Joan accompanied Charles to Reims, where he was crowned king in 1429.

However, the following year Joan was captured in battle and turned over to the English. Through their influence, she was accused of witchcraft and heresy and burned at the stake at Rouen on May 30, 1431 (her feast day). After a close examination of the records of her trial, in 1456 Pope Callistus III declared her to have been falsely condemned. She was canonized by Pope Benedict XV in 1920 and named the second patron saint of France, after St. Martin of Tours.*

Joan's canonization in the twentieth century is notable in an age in which the validity of holy wars and the idea of God's taking sides in war have been seriously questioned. What is most notable about Joan, however, is her absolute obedience to God and her submission to his will, especially at a time when it was unheard of for a woman to be garbed in men's clothes and lead an army into battle.

Jogues, St. Isaac (1607–46)

A fearless French Jesuit missionary, Jogues arrived in New France (Canada) in 1636 and traveled by canoe and foot, first to the Huron territory south of Lake Huron, and then three hundred miles northward to a place he named "Sault Sainte Marie." There, two thousand native people were converted, but a companion's ill health caused Jogues to return to Quebec in 1642.

His next mission was to the Iroquois, who hated the French after Champlain had defeated them at a battle near Ticonderoga in 1609. Jogues, along with René Goupil and others, was captured and enslaved by the Mohawks (an Iroquois tribe). Though his hands were maimed and he was tortured, Jogues sought to convert his captors until he escaped and returned to France.

After receiving special permission from Pope Urban VIII to say Mass in spite of his hand injuries, Jogues chose to return to the Mohawk mission. While among them as part of a peace delegation, he and a lay volunteer, Jean de Lalande, were treacherously killed by the Mohawks in 1646. However, their work among a hostile tribe was not in vain, as converts such as Blessed Kateri Tekakwitha* (the "Lily of the Mohawks") testify.

The faith and courage of these Jesuit martyr-missionaries of upstate New York—Isaac Jogues, René Goupil, and Jean de Lalande—led to their canonization by Pope Pius XI* in 1930 along with the other "North American Martyrs" of Canada (including St. Jean de Brébeuf*). A shrine to these martyrs in Auriesville, New York, where Jogues and Lalande were martyred, is a well-known pilgrimage site. (Feast, October 19.)

John Chrysostom, St. (c. 349–407)

This saint, whose blunt and fiery sermons were reminiscent of the prophets of the Old Testament, was dubbed "Golden Mouth" ("Chrysostom"). He was born and educated in Antioch, a wealthy Christian city. After he was baptized at age twenty, John served Bishop Meletius as an aide for three years and then began to live as a monk.

After four years in a monastery, he became a hermit and subjected himself to such austerity that his health was permanently impaired and he was forced to return to Antioch. John was ordained a deacon there and wrote treatises on various subjects. He humbly declined to be ordained a priest but finally deferred to the bishop's wishes in 386.

As a priest, John's reputation as a preacher grew over twelve years in Antioch. In 398 he was suddenly summoned to become the twelfth bishop of Constantinople. In this office he eliminated lavish entertainment and usually dined alone. He called his clergy to holiness.

The *Hagia Sophia*, John's cathedral, rang with his stirring homilies. He spoke on many themes: the good of marriage, the Christian's responsibility toward the poor, and the seductions of popular entertainment. Sadly, his denunciation of the errors of the Jews (common in his day) has an extremely anti-Semitic ring today, but his reputation was that of a champion of the poor and the common man.

John, however, was not a politician, and he aroused the ire of Theophilus, bishop of Alexandria, when he welcomed to Constantinople three monks (the so-called "Three Long Brothers") whom Theophilus had exiled because of their Origenist* theology. Chrysostom also preached sermons that offended the Roman empress Eudoxia (supposedly calling her a "Jezebel"). So the emperor conspired to have John denounced and exiled by calling the Synod of the Oak in 403.

As he was being exiled, a sign of divine disfavor (either an earthquake or the empress's miscarriage) caused the emperor to return John to his see, amidst great celebration among the people. But this triumph was short-lived, since John continued to speak boldly against abuses and the synod's sentence was still in force. This time, in 404, John was exiled to the farthest Eastern corner of the empire, where he died on a forced march.

The bishops of the East refused even to mention John's name in the official prayers for the dead (the *diptychs*) for twenty years. However, through appeals of the popes and the common people, John's sanctity was finally recognized. One of the great liturgies of the East now bears his name. (Feast, September 14.)

John of Capistrano, St. (1386–1456)

While imprisoned by hostile forces during his term as governor of Perugia, John heard God's call to become a Franciscan, which he did in 1416. He was an effective preacher; Pope Nicholas V sent him to Austria to convert the Hussites.* At age seventy, his preaching helped gather an army that defeated the Ottoman Turks at Belgrade in 1456 shortly before his death of the plague. (Feast, October 23.)

John of Monte Corvino (1247–1328)

This Franciscan priest was the first to preach the gospel in China. Pope Nicholas IV sent him to deliver letters to Kublai Khan. Arriving in India in 1291, he set out for China and arrived in 1294, just after Kublai Khan's death. However, the new khan welcomed him and allowed him to teach the Catholic faith. John built the first church in Beijing in 1299, welcomed other Franciscan missionaries, and was consecrated archbishop of Beijing in 1308.

John of the Cross, St. (1542–91)

As a boy, Juan de Yepes endured poverty, but through his widowed mother's efforts and God's providence he was able to study Latin and rhetoric in the evenings after serving the sick in a hospital. At twenty-one, he refused a hospital chaplain position to join the Carmelite order (1563). John excelled in both prayer and study, and within a few years was made prefect of studies of a college in Salamanca.

In his love for contemplation, John considered becoming a Carthusian monk, but his plans changed when, in 1567, he met St. Teresa of Avila.* She enlisted John to work with her in establishing reformed ("discalced") Carmelite houses for men, as she had been doing for women. After serving as novice master in the first discalced friars' houses, John joined Teresa as spiritual guide for the sisters at Avila for five years.

After these fruitful years, however, John was imprisoned for nine months in a dispute among the members of his order. Enduring extreme maltreatment, he then composed most of his poetic *Spiritual Canticle* before engineering a bold escape. After the discalced Carmelites were granted autonomy, John served peacefully as a college rector and prior of two houses successively. Nevertheless, his life was never far from suffering; he died of illness in 1591 after he was banished by his own Carmelite general.

John of the Cross, a name he chose for himself, is known as the mystic who best expressed how God is found in suffering and *nada* (nothingness). His education as a poet and philosopher lends particular eloquence and power to his works, which include *The Ascent of Mount Carmel*, *The Dark Night of the Soul*, and *The Living Flame of Love*. John was canonized in 1726 and declared a Doctor of the Church in 1926. (Feast, December 14.)

John Paul II, Pope (1920–)

Since his election to the papacy in 1978, the first non-Italian pope since Adrian VI in 1522, Karol Wojtyla has had a tremendous impact on both the Church and the world. As a youth growing up near Cracow, Poland, he enjoyed poetry and acting as well as outdoor sports. After the German invasion of Poland, he was part of an underground theater troupe and later entered an underground seminary.

Ordained in 1946, Wojtyla earned a doctorate in theology in Rome in 1948 and then, as a parish priest in Poland, earned a doctorate in philosophy from Lublin, where he also taught ethics beginning in 1956. He was made an auxiliary bishop of Cracow in 1958 and archbishop in 1963. He was an active participant in the Second Vatican Council,* where he helped draft the *Pastoral Constitution on the Church in the Modern World* (*Gaudium et Spes*). Appointed cardinal in 1967, Wojtyla worked against Communist oppression in Poland.

It was a surprise to him and to many when he was elected pope at age fifty-eight, succeeding John Paul I, whose papacy had lasted only thirty-one days. Immediately John Paul II began his task of continuing the faithful implementation of the Second Vatican Council*, which he said is the key for understanding his pontificate. His earlier writings (for example, *Love and Responsibility*) are reflected in his papal teachings, such as those on marriage and the family.

John Paul's teaching is based on profound respect for the dignity of the human person. Among his numerous encyclical letters, he discussed the special identity and mission of the three persons of the Blessed Trinity (*Redemptor Hominis*, 1978; *Dives et Misericordiae*, 1980; and *Dominum et Vivificantem*, 1986), social issues (*Laborem Exercens*, 1981, and *Centissimus Annus*, 1991), ecumenism (*Ut Unum Sint*, 1995), moral theology (*Veritatis Splendor*, 1993), life issues (*Evangelium Vitae*, 1995), faith and reason (*Fides et Ratio*, 1998), and the mission of the Church (*Redemptoris Missio*, 1990), among other topics.

As the most publicly visible and widely-traveled pope in history, John Paul has personally embodied the missionary dimension of the Church, always proclaiming the gospel with great hope, and inviting all to "open wide the doors to Christ." He has had a particular call to evangelize the youth of the world, holding many "World Youth Days."

On the global scene, John Paul has met with many world leaders. Many consider his influence a major factor in the breakup of the Soviet bloc in 1989. However, the nature of his influence was always to promote the values and teachings of the gospel, especially as expressed in the teachings of Vatican II.

John Paul's deep devotion to Mary is reflected in his motto: *Totus Tuus* ("Everything for you"). As he led the Catholic Church into the third millennium with the Great Jubilee Year (2000), he reminded the world once again that we are (to use the title of his 1994 book) *Crossing the Threshold of Hope* as we look to Jesus Christ alone as the Redeemer of the human race.

John XXIII, Blessed Pope (1881–1963)

One of the most beloved popes in the history of the papacy, Angelo Roncalli was also one of the most surprising. From simple peasant stock, Roncalli had served the Church in apostolic missions to Bulgaria, Turkey, Greece, and France before being appointed cardinal and patriarch of Venice in 1953, where he wrote five volumes on St. Charles Borromeo.* His election to the papacy in 1958 at age seventy-seven was a surprising one to many, but his warmth immediately endeared him to the Roman people and to the world.

John continued to expand and internationalize the College of Cardinals and wrote pastorally oriented encyclical letters on peace (*Pacem in Terris,* 1963) and social teaching (*Mater et Magistra,* 1961). But the great surprise of his papacy was his calling of the Second Vatican Council,* only the second ecumenical council in four hundred years. Even his own secretary of state did not take John seriously when he announced (on the feast of St. Paul's conversion, January 25, 1958), his intention to call the council.

Nevertheless, the preparatory commissions were soon set in motion. The theme of the council was to be *aggiornamento* (literally, "making up-to-date")—a council of renewal, and a council clearly intended by John not to condemn errors of the modern world, but to reach out to the world (including other Christians, non-Christians, Communists ... everyone!) with the liberating truth of the gospel of Christ. The Church was not to be presented as a closed society or institution, but as the people of God who are sent out by Christ to be the "light to the nations" (*Lumen Gentium,* the title of the council's central document) to present the "joy and hope" (*Gaudium et Spes,* another council document) of Christ to all.

John XXIII clearly presented this purpose to the bishops gathered in

Rome in his speech at the opening of the council in 1962. Though he died only eight months later, the council continued to carry out the program for renewal he set forth. His autobiography, *The Journey of a Soul*, is a powerful testimony of John's simple life and holiness. In 2000, Pope John Paul II* beatified him, along with Pope Pius IX,* who convened the First Vatican Council.

Joseph II (1741–90)

The Holy Roman Emperor from 1765 to 1790, Joseph was an "enlightened" ruler who claimed the right to regulate Church affairs, reform perceived abuses, and grant religious toleration to all in his realm. The practice of "Josephinism" (or "Josephism") was derived from the theory of Febronius ("Febronianism") that limited the authority of the pope in Church affairs and transferred this authority to the state. The Catholic Church suffered great harm from Joseph's policies through his seizure of monasteries, seminaries, and schools. Pope Pius VI vigorously opposed his policy, even traveling to Vienna to protest them in 1782, but with little effect. After Joseph's death and the French Revolution, the policy of Josephinism lost force in the nineteenth century.

Julian of Norwich (1342–c. 1413)

Dame Julian was an English mystic who wrote down a series of revelations or "showings" that she received on May 13, 1373. Though very little is known of her life other than that she was a recluse and contemplative, her writings indicate that she was either well educated or had received a gift of rhetoric from God. Her *Showings* primarily stress God's love, as seen in her insights into the Blessed Trinity and Christ's passion.

Justin Martyr, St. (c. 100–c. 165)

One of the famous Christian apologists (defenders of the faith) of the second century, Justin is the patron saint of philosophers. His quest for truth led him to examine the philosophies of the Stoics, Peripatetics, Pythagoreans, and Platonists. One day, though, while walking on the beach, he met an old man who simply shared with him the message of Jesus Christ. Justin became a Christian and found in Christ, the *Logos* (God's Reason and Word), the fulfillment of his philosophical quest for Truth.

Soon he turned his great intellect to studying the faith of Christ and to writing Christian apologies (explanations of the faith), both to Jews who had heard but not yet accepted Christ (the *Dialogue with Trypho the Jew*) and to the Romans (his *First* and *Second Apologies*). Many of his contemporaries labored under false conceptions of Christianity. They thought that Christians were atheists (for refusing to worship the Roman gods), cannibals (for eating the flesh of Christ), and sexually immoral (they thought their secret meetings for worship were really orgies). In Justin's apologies, he corrects these erroneous views, showing the beauty of the Catholic faith. He also gives a cogent summary of the Mass of his day, including many prayers from the Eucharistic canon.

When Justin was finally brought to trial for his faith, he gave bold witness to Jesus and was beheaded. (Feast, June 1.)

Justinian I (483–565)

This ruler has been called the first Byzantine emperor. During his long reign (527–65), he recaptured most of the empire's lands that had been conquered by foreign invaders. He saw himself as exercising spiritual as well as temporal authority (the policy called "Caesaropapism") and built the great church of Holy Wisdom, *Hagia* (or *Santa*) *Sophia* in Constantinople, as well as other basilicas.

Justinian called the Second Council of Constantinople* in 552 (which rejected Monophysitism) and codified Roman laws, creating the Code of Justinian. In spite of his successes, the great expense of his military campaigns drained his treasury, which caused revolts and left the Eastern empire weak just when the forces of Islam were emerging and poised to conquer the Byzantine empire in the next century.

Kant, Immanuel (1724–1804)

Kant was a renowned eighteenth-century Lutheran philosopher, whose works *Critique of Pure Reason* (first edition, 1781), *Critique of Practical Reason* (1788), and others revolutionized the philosophical world. Kant opposed traditional Catholic philosophy, such as the scholastic "proofs" of God's existence, and tried to re-found the philosophical basis for the assertion of God's existence in a universal moral law that is perceived through conscience and acted on in freedom.

Kino, Eusebio (1645–1711)

Born in Segno, Italy, Kino joined the Society of Jesus at twenty, studied in Bavaria, and set off to Mexico in 1678 as a missionary. His first mission field was lower (Baja) California. He loved the native peoples, and his one desire was to lead them to knowledge of Christ.

Kino's main missionary work began in 1687 when he established a mission (Dolores) in Pimeria Alta (now northern Sonora and southern Arizona), where he labored for twenty-four years, until 1711. He was a rancher and an explorer (producing the first maps of the region), but first a missionary, who established numerous missions throughout the region among the native peoples. Among the Pima Indians, Kino was known as "the Great White Father."

They loved him, he loved them, and they were willing to die for each other. He helped the Pimas protect themselves against hostile tribes. His endurance is legendary—he rode thirty or more miles a day for months at a time, stopping to preach and baptize the native peoples and to say Mass. He went on forty such missions, often alone, into harsh, unexplored territory. After a heroic life of preaching, prayer, humility, and poverty, Kino died at age sixty-six at one of his missions, St. Magdalene, which he had consecrated to his adopted patron saint, Francis Xavier.*

Kolbe, St. Maximilian (1894–1941)

The precocious Raymond Kolbe was only ten when (in 1904) the Virgin Mary appeared to him near his poor family home in Poland holding two crowns: the crown of purity and the crown of martyrdom. When Mary asked him to choose, Raymond boldly responded, "I choose both!"

The crown of purity was evident

early in his life, as Raymond followed Christ and entered the Franciscan order in 1911, taking the name Maximilian. In 1917 he was ordained and founded a Marian movement of prayer and evangelization, the "Militia Immaculata." The movement spread, especially through tracts and literature, including Kolbe's highly successful magazine, *Knight of the Immaculata* (1922).

Friars joined him in this mission of evangelization, and in 1927 Kolbe formed in Poland what was to become by 1935 the world's largest friary, Niepokalanow. In spite of very poor health (he had tuberculosis), Maximilian traveled to Japan and India, founding similar friaries that centered on prayer but also used modern means of communication to spread the gospel.

Soon after his return to Poland, the Nazis invaded his homeland in 1939, and after his second arrest, Maximilian was sent to the Auschwitz death camp. The crown of martyrdom was granted him when he boldly volunteered to go into a starvation bunker in place of a married man with children. As he had throughout his time in Auschwitz, Maximilian sang, prayed, heard confessions, and encouraged his fellow prisoners in the bunker, until he was given a lethal injection. The man whose life he had saved was present at both Maximilian's beatification and his canonization by the saint's fellow Pole, Pope John Paul II,* in 1982. (Feast, August 14.)

de Lamennais, Félicité (1782–1854)
One of the most original social thinkers of the nineteenth century, Lamennais was converted to the Catholic faith in 1804 largely due to the efforts of his brother, a priest. Lamennais himself was ordained in 1816 and became the architect of the French "Liberal Catholic" movement. He advocated freedom of the press and of religion, as well as the complete separation of Church and state.

Lamennais was "ultramontane"—looking to the pope to provide strong leadership to Catholics. He became the most prominent French clergyman of his day, and Pope Leo XII considered making him a cardinal. With Henri Lacordaire and Charles de Montalembert, Lamennais founded a newspaper, *L'Avenir* (*The Future*), in which he espoused the ideal of religious liberty, which was to be respected by the state and promoted by the pope.

However, Pope Gregory XVI did not share Lamennais' vision, ordering the paper's suspension and condemning many of Lamennais' positions in his encyclical *Mirari Vos* (1832). When Lamennais' apocalyptic book *Paroles d'un croyan* was condemned by the pope in 1834 (in *Singulari nos*),

Lamennais left the Catholic Church, despite the attempts of the new pope, Pius IX,* to reconcile him. His followers, Montalembert and Lacordaire, submitted and remained active Catholics. However, Lamennais' condemnation in 1834 effectively put an end to the Liberal Catholic movement, although its essential concept of religious liberty later was embraced by the Second Vatican Council.*

de La Salle, St. John Baptiste (1651–1719)
Founder of the "Christian Brothers" (Institute of the Brothers of Christian Schools), John was born into a noble family in Reims (France) in 1651 and was ordained a priest in 1678. In 1684, he gave his share of the family fortune to the poor and devoted himself to forming a community of teachers to educate poor boys: the Brothers of Christian Schools (F.S.C.). By 1694 he had drawn up his first rule for his lay brothers. His work spread to England and Italy and eventually to the New World.

John was a pioneering educator. He wrote *The Conduct of Christian Schools* and established training colleges for teachers as well as schools. His boarding school at Saint-Yon (established 1705) has served as a model for modern secondary education. He was canonized in 1900. (Feast, April 7.)

Lateran Council, Third (1179)

Pope Alexander III presided over this impressive council, which called for a two-thirds vote of cardinals to elect a pope, a crusade against the Albigensians* (an austere, dualistic movement in Germany and southern France), support of universities and cathedral schools, and other internal reform decrees.

Lateran Council, Fourth (1215)

The twelfth ecumenical council of the Catholic Church, this was the most important council of the Middle Ages in both its immediate and its long-term effects on the Church. Called by Pope Innocent III* at the height of his power, it was attended by over twelve hundred prelates. The council promulgated seventy decrees. The doctrine of transubstantiation was defined, the "Easter duty" (which requires Catholics to go to Confession and receive Holy Communion at least annually) was established, heresies were condemned, and bishops were given directives about reform within their dioceses and reminded of their duty to preach. The council also forbade the founding of religious communities with new rules and ordered distinctive attire for Jews and Muslims in Christian lands.

Lateran Council, Fifth (1512–17)

Pope Julius II convoked this eighteenth ecumenical council to denounce the decrees of an illicit council at Pisa called by French King Louis XII. Although some minor reform measures were also promulgated by this council, it failed to address the serious issues of reform of the Catholic Church that were soon to be raised by the Protestant reformers.

Lawrence, St. (d. 258)

One of the most famous martyrs of the early Church, Lawrence died in Valerian's persecution. He was one of the seven deacons of Rome under Pope St. Sixtus II (pope 257–58), who was captured while saying Mass in the catacombs of St. Callistus* and then beheaded and buried there. Shortly thereafter Lawrence was captured and repeatedly ordered to turn over the treasures of the Church to the Roman authorities.

The tradition holds that when Lawrence gathered the poor of Rome and presented them as the "treasures of the Church," he was summarily ordered to be roasted alive on a gridiron. The story of his courage and humor ("Turn me over," he quipped, "I'm done on this side") helped to promote his veneration by the faithful. (Feast, August 10.)

Leo I (the Great), Pope St. (d. 461)
History has bestowed the title "great" on two popes, and the courage, wisdom, and authority of Leo testify to his greatness. A Roman by birth, he served as a deacon of Rome under two popes and was elevated to the papacy in 440. First and foremost he was a pastor, whose direct, clear homilies elucidated the meaning of doctrine (especially the Incarnation) and addressed issues ranging from social justice and almsgiving to proper devotion to the saints. He also wrote to bishops opposing heresies (Manicheanism, Pelagianism,* Priscillianism, Nestorianism*) and admonishing them on personal matters.

Leo was also "great" in his courage in the social and political order. As the Roman Empire, especially in the West, had disintegrated and become virtually defenseless against the attacks of invading peoples, the Christian bishops increasingly took on the mantle of political leadership. Hence in 452, Pope Leo went out and convinced the fearsome Attila and his Huns not to invade Rome. Three years later, Leo could not prevent Genseric the Vandal from plundering the city, but he saved the lives of the populace and worked to rebuild the city and the churches. He also sent missionaries after Genseric to minister to those he had captured.

The greatest theological debate of the day was over the union of the two natures of Christ. At the request of Patriarch (Archbishop) Flavian of Constantinople, Leo wrote a famous letter (the *Tome of Leo*) condemning the teaching of the monk Eutyches,* which claimed that Jesus had only one nature, the divine nature. When this letter was ignored at a council in Ephesus in 449, Leo denounced the council as a *"latrocinium"*—a "robber council."

Leo's cry was heeded: Two years later at the Council of Chalcedon,* Eutyches' theology was condemned and Leo's tome was used in the Church's Christological definition. When the tome was read at Chalcedon, the bishops cried out: "This is the faith of the Church! Peter has spoken through Leo!"

By the time of his death in 460, Pope Leo had not only served his people and the Church well; he had raised the influence of the papacy to new heights. He was declared a Doctor of the Church in 1754. (Feast, September 10.)

Leo X, Pope (1475–1521)

A member of the wealthy dé Medici family, Leo X focused his pontificate (1513–21) on lavishly supporting Renaissance art and architecture, such as continuing the construction of St. Peter's Basilica in Rome. To fund these projects, Leo offered indulgences to those who contributed through authorized representatives. This scandalized Augustinian scholar Martin Luther* in Germany, and the conflict eventually led to Leo's excommunication of Luther in 1521. The pope's failure to recognize the necessity and urgency of reform in the Church contributed to the Protestant Reformation.

Leo XIII, Pope (1810–1903)

After his ordination to the priesthood in 1837, Vincenzo Pecci gained diplomatic experience in Brussels (as nuncio), London, Paris, Cologne, and elsewhere before being made bishop of Perugia in 1846. When he was elected to the papacy in 1878 at age sixty-eight, many thought he would be an "interim" pope. Instead, Leo reigned twenty-five years and ushered in the twentieth century.

While Blessed Pope Pius IX,* Leo's predecessor, was said to have made war on modern civilization, Leo was more conciliatory while still holding to tradition. He promoted the study of St. Thomas Aquinas* in *Aeterni Patris* (1879), making it the core of seminary training. Yet he also opened the Vatican archives to secular researchers in 1883 and gave a qualified affirmation of critical biblical scholarship—issuing *Providentissimus Deus* in 1893 and founding the Pontifical Biblical Commission in 1902. He sought to restore Christian unity, while also declaring Anglican holy orders to be invalid (*Apostolicae Curae*, 1896).

In international relations, he improved the Church's relationship with most European nations, notably ending Bismarck's *Kulturkampf* ("culture war") against the Church. But he was distressed by France's growing anti-Catholicism and anticlericalism and Italy's prohibition against Catholics participating in Italian politics. In addition, Leo had a truly global view of the Church, establishing 248 new dioceses worldwide, including twenty-eight in the United States.

While promoting many traditional and new Catholic devotions—devotion to Christ in the Eucharist, to Mary and the rosary, to the Sacred Heart of Jesus, and to the Holy Spirit—Leo is best known for his progressive social teaching, publishing the first modern Catholic social encyclical, *Rerum Novarum*, in 1891. This document emphasizes the responsibility of

Christians for the social order. While taking a more positive approach to the world, Leo also condemned communism, socialism, and the so-called "Americanist" heresy. In many ways, Leo is a model pope for our times, as he sought to bring forth in the Church treasures "old and new" (see Mt 13:52).

Liguori, St. Alphonsus (1696–1787)

Son of a wealthy nobleman in Naples, Alphonsus Liguori became a doctor of civil and canon law at age sixteen. However, in his eighth year of practice, humiliated in losing an important case, Alphonsus gave up law to become a priest. In spite of severe asthma and his father's opposition, Alphonsus was ordained in 1726 and became a celebrated preacher.

In 1731, he took over the reform of a community of religious women. In 1732 he founded the Congregation of the Most Holy Redeemer (Redemptorists), devoted to preaching and missionary work among the rural poor. Ironically, due to internal strife he was expelled for a time from the order he founded.

Liguori's other great contributions were in moral theology and devotional works. He countered the moral rigorism that the Jansenists* had planted in France, stressing the readiness of Christ to forgive the sinner. His two-volume *Moral Theology* is a classic, and his devotional writings, including *The Way of Salvation, True Spouse of Jesus Christ,* and *The Glories of Mary,* were widely read and later translated into over sixty languages.

Liguori also served as the bishop of a poor diocese from 1762–75. Pope Pius IX* declared him a Doctor of the Church in 1871, and in 1950 he was named patron of confessors and moral theologians by Pope Pius XII.* (Feast, August 1.)

Loisy, Alfred (1857–1940)

The "father of modernism," Loisy was a Frenchman ordained a priest in 1879 and later serving as a professor of Scripture at the Institute Catholique in Paris. Questionable doctrinal teaching caused his dismissal from this post, but he continued to explore the development of the Bible and the history of doctrine. Loisy published *The Gospel and the Church* (1903) to show that the Catholic Church was a true and legitimate development of Christ's teaching (refuting Adolph von Harnack), but the book was condemned for various errors and placed on the Index of Forbidden Books.

At first Loisy submitted, but after Pope Pius X* issued his two antimodernist documents of 1907, Loisy renounced the Catholic Church and was excommunicated in 1908. He taught history of religion at the Collége de France from 1909–30.

Lonergan, Bernard (1904–84)

A Canadian Jesuit priest, Lonergan was one of the primary "transcendental Thomists" along with fellow Jesuits Karl Rahner* and Joseph Maréchal. Lonergan did an innovative study in human understanding, *Insight* (1957), and authored *Method in Theology* (1972). After a teaching career marked by illness in later life, he died in 1984.

Louis IX, King St. (1214–70)

The model Christian king, Louis ruled France from 1226 to 1270, though his first years were under the regency of his mother, Blessed Blanche of Castille. His wife, Margaret of Provence, bore him eleven children.

Louis joined the Third Order of St. Francis,* a commitment reflected throughout his reign by his concern for the poor, for justice (that every man should have his due), and for lasting peace within and among nations. However, Louis also embraced the crusader ideal of liberation of the Holy Land for Christian pilgrims. He led two ill-fated crusades: the Seventh Crusade* (1248–54), in which he was

captured and had to be ransomed, and the Eighth Crusade* (1270), during which he died of the plague with his son in 1270.

Besides his work to ensure justice and reform of government administration, Louis was a patron of the Church; he built, for example, the Saint-Chapelle in Paris to enshrine Jesus' crown of thorns, a gift from Emperor Baldwin II. He was also a patron of education; he supported, for example, the Sorbonne Theological College. His personal piety and austerity also contributed to his rapid canonization by Pope Boniface VIII* in 1297. (Feast, August 25.)

Lubich, Chiara (1920–)

Lubich, an Italian, founded the Focalare movement in 1943, which was approved by Rome in 1962. Although there are many different branches of this Catholic renewal movement (for celibates who work in the world, married people, youth, and priests), the common purpose of the movement is to change the world by living the gospel in a radical, joyful way in ordinary circumstances. The annual meetings of the movement, called "Mariopolis" ("City of Mary"), are held worldwide.

Luther, Martin (1483–1546)

Luther, founder of the Protestant Reformation, joined the Augustinian hermits in 1505 and was ordained a Catholic priest in 1507. Despite his penitential life and recourse to the sacraments, he failed to sense God's merciful forgiveness. As he worked toward a doctorate in Scripture, he became increasingly critical of the Catholic Church's interpretation of justification and of the "selling" of indulgences.

On October 31, 1517, Luther posted the famous "Ninety-Five Theses on Indulgences" on the door of the castle church in Wittenburg (where he taught), inviting others to debate this issue with him. He was called to explain his teaching before Cardinal Thomas Cajetan at Augsburg and Johannes Eck at Leipzig. These debates only alienated Luther further from the Catholic Church. When his teachings were condemned by Pope Leo X* in *Exsurge Domine* on June 12, 1520, Luther responded by burning the bull and other Catholic books, resulting in his excommunication from the Catholic Church on January 3, 1521.

Lwanga, St. Charles (d. 1886)

The missionary White Fathers had brought the Catholic faith to Uganda in 1879, and one of their most fervent converts was a royal page in the king's court, Charles Lwanga. After being baptized in 1885, Lwanga sought to convert his fellow pages to Christ, until King Mtesa found their purity an affront to his own decadent lifestyle. Some advisors took the opportunity to convince the king to "purify" the country by purging it of Christians.

Mtesa proceeded to execute his Christian prime minister, expel all foreign priests, and then turn on Charles Lwanga and twenty other pages who publicly declared themselves to be Christians. They were taken on a death march and executed, one by one, at each village, until the final group, including Lwanga, was tortured and burned to death. The peace of these martyrs, praying and witnessing to Christ to the end, was a powerful witness. They were canonized by Pope Paul VI* in 1964. (Feast, June 3.)

Lyons, Second Council of (1274)

This fourteenth ecumenical council of the Catholic Church sought to reestablish the unity of the Church. It was attended by more than five hundred bishops and by noted theologians St. Bonaventure* and St. Albertus Magnus.* At the council, the Orthodox delegates of Emperor Michael VIII Palaelogus accepted papal authority and Western articles of faith. The union declared by this council, however, was short-lived, lasting only until 1289. There was simply not enough support for reunion in the Eastern churches.

Macrina, St. (d. 380)

Macrina, the sister of St. Gregory of Nyssa* and St. Basil,* is known to us through her brother Gregory's biography and through the dialogue with her brother, *On the Soul and the Resurrection*, that reportedly occurred soon before her death. She had a significant impact on the Church of her age.

Macrina is remarkable for the personal influence she had on others. After deciding to dedicate herself to Christ as a celibate, she convinced her mother to follow her example. Then she persuaded her brother Basil to abandon a promising career in rhetoric to pursue the ascetic life, which he did. Finally, she founded and led a women's religious community. (Feast, July 19.)

Martel, Charles (c. 690–741)

Son of Pepin II of Heristal, "Charles the Hammer" established the authority of his family dynasty (called "Pippinid" or later "Carolingian") over the Frankish kingdom and surrounding lands during his rule (719–41). With regard to the Church, he was a patron of Anglo-Saxon missionaries St. Willibrord, bishop of Utrecht (in Frisia), and later of St. Boniface*, archbishop of Mainz. This support paved the way for the important alliance between the papacy and the Frankish rulers. Charles is also famous for his defeat of Muslim forces at the battle of Tours in 732, which prevented the birth of an Islamic nation of Western Europe.

Martin I, Pope St. (d. 655)

This courageous pope is considered the last pope to suffer martyrdom for his defense of the Catholic faith. When he steadfastly refused to accept the doctrine that Jesus has only one will (the Monothelite heresy), the Byzantine emperor Constans II arrested him, dragged him from Rome to Constantinople, convicted him of treason, and finally sent the elderly, ill Martin to die in exile in 655. Adding to Martin's suffering, the church in Rome sent no relief to him, and even (contrary to his expressed will) elected a new pope to succeed him after Constans deposed him in 653, two years before he died. However, Martin's stand was not in vain; twenty-five years after his death, the Third Council of Constantinople* (the sixth ecumenical council) was convened and repeated Martin's condemnation of the Monothelite heresy. (Feast, April 13.)

Martin of Tours, St. (d. 397)

Martin was the earliest saint to be honored throughout Europe. His universal popularity could be attributed to the well-known story of Martin's dividing his military cloak to give half of it to a beggar. However, this was only the beginning of Martin's life as a Christian. After his conversion and discharge from the army, he preached to his pagan parents (who were converted) and then lived as a hermit while the persecution of the Arian* emperor, Constantius II, raged.

When Bishop Hilary of Poitiers* returned from exile, he enlisted Martin to found the first monastery in the West, at Liège, in 361. In 371 the people of Tours acclaimed him as their bishop. He lived at the monastery of Marmoutier and served as bishop with zeal and great simplicity and charity. He was said to possess a gift of healing, which supplemented all his charitable work with prisoners and the needy. His feast day (November 11) was the original Thanksgiving day in Europe for a bountiful harvest, and many still celebrate that day with a "St. Martin's goose." (Feast, November 11.)

Martyrs of Lyons and Vienne (second century)

The ancient accounts of martyrs' deaths won sympathy for Christians, but more importantly, they won converts and stirred up the faith and zeal of the Church. In his *History of the Church*, Eusebius of Caesarea* includes a letter addressed to "brethren in Asia and Phrygia" recounting the martyrdoms that occurred in southern Gaul around 177. About fifty Christians perished. After they had been beaten, humiliated, and rounded up by an angry mob, they were sent to death by the governor simply upon their admission that they were Christians.

The account focuses on the heroism and suffering of a young, seemingly delicate slave girl, St. Blandina, who grew stronger each time she professed, "I am a Christian, and with us no evil finds a place." Also noted is the constancy of the ninety-year-old bishop, St. Ponthinus, who was succeeded after the persecution by St. Irenaeus.*

Melito of Sardis, St. (d. c. 190)

In an apologetic work addressed to the Roman emperor Marcus Aurelius around 170, Bishop Melito tried to convince the emperor that Christianity and the Roman state had common interests. Jesus Christ and the emperor were like "fraternal twins," he said, as they both appreciated the good of true religion and the peace of the state. This claim prophesied the unity of Christianity and the state that would begin with Constantine* two centuries later.

Melito is also known for his powerful "Easter Homily on the Passover," the most ancient Christian Paschal homily preserved. It shows how the Exodus account (see Ex 12) prefigures Christ's Passover from death to resurrection. He is "the Passover of our salvation." (Feast, April 1.)

Merici, St. Angela (c. 1470–1540)
Among the religious congregations founded in the period of the Catholic reformation, the "Ursulines," named after its founder's patron, St. Ursula, shines brightly. Angela was a Third Order Franciscan* in her early years. While on pilgrimage in the Holy Land in 1524–25, she was temporarily blinded and soon afterwards had visions that led her to found the Ursulines in 1535. It is the oldest teaching order of women in the Church. Angela was elected superior of the order in 1537, but died in 1540. (Feast, January 27.)

Merton, Thomas (1915–1968)
A brilliant but searching young man, Merton eventually found Christ and became a Cistercian monk in 1941 at Gethsemani Abbey, Kentucky. He became well known through his autobiography, *The Seven Storey Mountain*, but was also widely respected as a spiritual writer, poet, mystic, and prophet of non-violence. He died of accidental electrocution while visiting Bangkok, Thailand, in 1968.

Michelangelo Buonarroti (1475–1564)
Michelangelo represents the great glory of Renaissance art, carried out (at least in part) through the patronage of the popes. He was apprenticed in Florence in the house of a wealthy and influential Medici family. There he was schooled not only in art, but also in poetry, literature, and philosophy.

Michelangelo's great love was sculpture (the *Pieta, David, Moses*), but Pope Julius II enlisted him to paint the ceiling of the Sistine Chapel in the Vatican. Later, under Pope Paul III,* he painted frescos in the Pauline Chapel and served as chief architect of St. Peter's Basilica in Rome. He died in Rome on February 18, 1564.

Miki, St. Paul (1562–97)
Born into a noble family of the Samurai clan in Japan, Paul was educated by the Jesuits and joined their order in 1580. He was known to be a powerful evangelist and teacher, and so when the government launched a persecution against Christianity, Paul and twenty-five others were arrested and

condemned to death. They were crucified on the "Hill of Martyrs" overlooking Nagasaki bay, while boldly professing their faith and hope in Jesus. Pope Pius IX* canonized Paul and his companions in 1862. (Feast, February 6.)

Möhler, Johann Adam (1796–1838)

Möhler was a German Catholic priest and a leader of the Catholic Tübingen theological school. As a professor of Church history at Tübingen, Germany, beginning in 1828 (later at Münich), he propounded a view of the Church as a vital, Spirit-filled community—more like a living organism than an institution. Some have viewed Möhler's ecclesiology as anticipating the Second Vatican* Council, while others claim that he was a "proto-modernist." He wrote a famous book on finding Christ in the Church, *Symbolik*, as well as books on the oneness of the Church, the life of St. Athanasius,* a commentary on Romans, and a Church history.

de Molinos, Miguel (1628–96)

Molinos was a seventeenth-century Spanish priest known as the father of Quietism,* a spirituality advocating an openness to God through total contemplative passivity. His major work

was the *Spiritual Guide* (1675). In spite of his reputation as a spiritual director and his influential friends in the Roman Curia, Molinos was tried and condemned for heresy in 1687. He was imprisoned for the last nine years of his life. Nonetheless, his teaching influenced the Quietist movement in France (led by Madame Guyon* and Archbishop Fénelon*) and the Pietists.

Monica, St. (331–87)

The mother of St. Augustine,* Monica was instrumental in his conversion, as well as that of her husband, Patricius, through her persistent prayers. In his autobiography *The Confessions*, Augustine wrote of her, "I thought that you [God] were silent and that it was my mother who was speaking; but you were not silent; you spoke to me through her" (2, 3).

Augustine also quotes her words to him at Ostia, after his conversion and shortly before her death: "Son, as far as I am concerned, nothing in this life now gives me any pleasure.... I did have one reason for wanting to live a little longer: to see you become a Catholic Christian before I died. God has lavished his gifts on me in that respect, for I know that you have even renounced earthly happiness to be his servant." Not surprisingly, Monica is honored as a model of the power of intercessory prayer, especially prayer for conversion. (Feast, August 27.)

Montanism

Restoration of the Pauline gifts of the Holy Spirit (especially prophecy) and strict asceticism was the program of this movement, which emerged in the latter half of the second century. Montanus, a priest in Phrygia (Asia Minor), perceived that the love and zeal of the Church were growing cold and felt an urgency to restore these qualities before the imminent return of the Lord. The prophecies uttered by him and two prophetesses of his congregation were promulgated widely and were considered by his followers, the "Montanists," to be of an authority comparable to sacred Scripture. This belief, along with the imposition of stricter fasting regulations than required by the Church, led the bishops of the region to warn against the movement and finally to condemn it when Montanus and his followers refused to submit to their judgments.

The movement might have dissolved rapidly had it not been for the support of its most prominent convert, the great North African lawyer and apologist Tertullian.* After his death, Montanism gradually died out in the third century. But it left the Church

with unresolved questions about the proper use of the gifts of the Holy Spirit (charisms) in the Church and the possibility of stricter asceticism for some Christians in the Church. The Montanist movement's error was to impose adherence to its prophecies and fasting regulation as mandatory for all true ("spiritual") Christians.

More, St. Thomas (1478–1535)

Truly one of the most remarkable men of his time, More received a sound classical education and engaged in dialogue with humanist scholars John Colet and Desiderius Erasmus,* among others. After testing a religious vocation, More decided to pursue legal studies and rose steadily in public office until King Henry VIII* appointed him the lord chancellor of England in 1529. He accepted this position on the condition that he would be exempt from involvement in the king's pursuit of a divorce from his wife, Catherine of Aragon.

Nevertheless, this neutrality proved impossible. More was forced to resign as chancellor in 1532 and sought a quiet retirement with his income cut off by the king. Though More had helped compose Henry's *Assertion of the Seven Sacraments* against Martin Luther,* Henry now saw More as a bitter enemy because of More's refusal to accept the "Act of Supremacy," which declared Henry the head of the church in England. This hostility finally led to More's execution (after a conviction probably based on perjured testimony) on July 6, 1535.

More is known for his many writings, beginning with *Utopia* (1516) and ending with *Dialogue of Comfort Against Tribulation* and *Treatise upon the Passion;* these last two works were written in his final days while imprisoned in the Tower of London. But he is best remembered today for his fidelity to God and to his conscience, which resulted in his martyrdom. More's life is powerfully portrayed in Robert Bolt's twentieth-century play *A Man for All Seasons.* He is the patron saint of lawyers. (Feast, with fellow martyr St. John Fisher,* June 22.)

Mozart, Wolfgang Amadeus (1756–91)

This eighteenth-century Austrian composer produced over twenty Masses, eighteen organ sonatas for use during Mass, and many well-known individual works such as *Ave Verum* and *Exsultate, Jubilate.* The maturity and exuberance of his works made them an ideal example of later Baroque Catholic musical expression.

Murray, John Courtney (1904–67)

Murray was an American Jesuit priest whose works on religious liberty, such as *We Hold These Truths,* were influential in the drafting of the *Declaration on Religious Freedom* (*Dignitatis Humanae*) at the Second Vatican* Council.

N

Neri, St. Philip (1515–95)

A saint whose life abounded in the joy of the Holy Spirit, Neri was founder of the Roman Oratory and known as the "Apostle of Rome." He was one of the greatest figures of the Catholic Reformation.

As a boy, he was known by all in his hometown of Florence as *"Pippo buono"*—"good Philip"—who was always full of good cheer and charity. At age eighteen, he left Florence forever to work for his uncle as a businessman. But after a few months Philip decided to abandon a prosperous life in order to follow Christ; he left all and went to Rome.

Philip made a meager living as a tutor and frequently went on pilgrimages to Rome's "seven churches," often praying all night. One night in 1544 when he was praying in the catacombs of St. Sebastian, the Holy Spirit entered into him as a visible ball of fire. His heart literally expanded (his autopsy revealed several ribs bent outward around it), and soon afterwards he began a powerful apostolate to lay and religious that became known as his Oratory. Oratory members met regularly to study Scripture, Church history, and the lives of the saints, and then went out (often singing) to visit churches to pray or to serve the poor and sick in hospitals.

Though he resisted Holy Orders out of humility, Philip was eventually ordained due to the appeals and prayers of his friends. Already widely respected as a spiritual director, Philip became a sought-after confessor as well. After a period of trial in which his work and character were attacked by some men of influence, his love and straightforwardness resulted in his vindication and the conversion of his former enemies.

Philip desired to become a contemplative or a missionary, but God told him that Rome was his "desert" and his "India." There he remained to the end of his life, a spiritual advisor to many cardinals and other Church leaders. Meanwhile, his Oratories spread throughout Italy. (Feast, May 26.)

Nestorius (d. c. 451)

This controversial figure emerged from an ascetic life near Antioch when emperor Theodosius II named him archbishop of Constantinople in 428. He objected to honoring Mary with the title *Theotokos* ("God-bearer" or "Mother of God"), claiming that this phrase confused Christ's divine and human natures. Pope St. Celestine of Rome and St. Cyril of Alexandria* strenuously objected to this stand, which led to the condemnation of "Nestorianism" and the deposition of Nestorius by the Council of Ephesus in 431. This council affirmed that Mary could be honored as the "Mother of God" because she bore the one Person, Jesus Christ, who is both fully human and fully divine.

In exile, Nestorius wrote a treatise (the *Bazaar of Heracleides*) claiming that he agreed with the later definition of the Council of Chalcedon* that Christ was "one person in two natures" and disavowing the belief of the "Nestorian" churches that the divine Christ and the human Jesus were two different persons.

Neumann, St. John Nepomucene (1811–60)

Neumann was born in Bohemia and received a seminary education in Budweis and Prague. Always seeking to serve God and unconcerned with his own welfare or reputation, he came to America in 1836 with little money and no direction. The bishop of New York City, in need of priests, ordained him and sent him to Buffalo, New York, to minister to German-speaking immigrants.

Sensing God's call to religious life, Neumann joined the Redemptorist order in 1842. As his Redemptorist novitiate, he traveled thousands of miles in and around Pittsburgh ministering to people. He was later assigned to a Redemptorist parish in Baltimore and quite unexpectedly chosen to be the bishop of Philadelphia in 1852.

Though he found administration tedious, Neumann worked tirelessly to upgrade Catholic education and build churches and schools in Philadelphia. He had a major role in the First Council of Baltimore in 1852 and was called to Rome in 1854 for the definition of the Immaculate Conception. He was known as a pastor who loved nothing more than to administer the sacraments to his people and to pray. He promoted the Forty Hours devotion and often spent his day off at a Redemptorist house, even helping the lay brothers in the kitchen. He died of a heart attack at age forty-nine in 1860 and was canonized by Pope Paul VI* in 1977. (Feast, January 5.)

Newman, Venerable John Henry (1801–90)

Newman is one of the most significant religious thinkers of the nineteenth century and its most prominent convert to Catholicism. His youth in London was absorbed with a religious quest that finally led him to embrace the Anglican faith of his parents as a student at Oxford. At Oriel College, he studied for the priesthood and was ordained an Anglican priest in 1824. From 1828 to 1841 he was vicar of St. Mary's College, Oxford, and his sermons (published as *Parochial and Plain Sermons*) influenced the religious life of Oxford and the whole country. He grew very ill in 1832 and took a Mediterranean voyage, composing on the voyage his famous poem "Lead, Kindly Light."

Newman's study of the fathers of the early Church, which resulted in the publication of *The Arians of the Fourth Century* (1833), eventually led him to become a leader of the Oxford Movement (also known as the Tractarian movement, after the movement's *Tracts for the Times,* published from 1833 to 1841). This movement advocated the freedom of the Anglican church from political manipulation and viewed Anglicanism as the *via media* (middle way) between the "extremes" of Protestantism and Roman Catholicism. However, Newman's studies produced in him a growing uneasiness and suspicion that the *via media* was just a "paper theory" that did not match the historical evidence of the Church's actual life and growth.

The watershed event was the publication of Newman's *Tract 90,* in which he claimed that the Thirty-Nine Articles, the basis of the Church of England, did not contradict the actual teaching of the Catholic Church. In the ensuing Anglican outcry against Newman, he resigned from St. Mary's and went into semi-monastic seclusion at Littlemore, near Oxford. In 1843 he preached a farewell sermon at Littlemore, "The Parting of Friends," and two years later was received into the Catholic Church by an Italian Passionist priest.

Newman's public life as a Catholic began with his publication of *An Essay on the Development of Christian Doctrine* (1845), which explains how the Catholic Church has changed through an organic growth. He was ordained a Catholic priest in 1847 and joined the Congregation of the Oratory of St. Philip Neri,* establishing oratories in Birmingham and London. Based on the principles articulated in *The Idea of a University* (1852), he served as first rector of the Catholic University of Dublin (1851–58).

When Newman returned to England, he spent the rest of his life in preaching, study, writing, and priestly ministry. In *Apologia Pro Vita Sua* (1864), his famous religious autobiography, Newman defended himself from

Charles Kingsley's charges of duplicity with regard to his conversion. The height of his theoretical writing was *The Grammar of Assent* (1870), in which he explored the nature of faith and assent to truth. He also wrote poems ("The Dream of Gerontius," 1866), and novels (*Loss and Gain*, 1848, and *Callista*, 1856). He served briefly as editor of *The Rambler*, in which he wrote a controversial article "On Consulting the Faithful in Matters of Doctrine."

Newman's life as a Roman Catholic was not easy. He was isolated in a largely Anglican country, and his Catholic positions were not always appreciated or understood even by Catholics. He opposed, for example, the defining of papal infallibility at Vatican I, but fully embraced it once it was defined.

Newman's teachings were novel, but suspicions about his "liberalism" were quieted when Pope Leo XIII* made him a cardinal in 1879. His mottos, "Out of the shadows and images and into the truth" and "Heart speaks to heart," have inspired many. In the twentieth century, Newman's theology has been more fully appreciated as anticipating the teachings of Vatican II.* He was declared "Venerable" by Pope John Paul II* in 1991.

Nicea, First Council of (325)

The symbolic number of "318 white-robed elders" (see Gn 14:14)—actually 220 to 250 bishops—were summoned by the emperor Constantine* to settle the controversy over the teaching of the Alexandrine presbyter, Arius.* Arianism was condemned, as the creed* formulated by the council fathers professed the full divinity of God the Son and his unity and equality with the Father, as expressed in the Greek term *homoousious* ("of the same substance" or "one in being"). Since the Catholic belief in the divine guidance of the ecumenical councils in defining doctrine was not yet established, some bishops later questioned the authority of the teaching of this first ecumenical ("worldwide" or "universal") council of the Catholic Church. The council's condemnation of Arianism was reaffirmed by the First Council of Constantinople* in 381.

Nicea, Second Council of (787)

The seventh ecumenical council of the Church was called by the empress Irene to settle the issue of whether it was valid to use and venerate sacred images (icons). Despite the disruption by Iconoclast soldiers of the council's first attempt to convene in 786, the uprising was suppressed and the council met in 787. The council fathers upheld the validity of the proper veneration (not worship) of various kinds of sacred images, and the Iconoclasts ("image breakers") were condemned.

Nicholas of Cusa (1401–64)

Nicholas was a prominent fifteenth-century philosopher, Church leader, and mystic. Trained as a canon lawyer in Padua, he became well known at the Council of Basle in 1433, where he worked for the reconciliation of moderate Hussites* (known as Calixtines or Utraquists) to the Catholic Church. He also worked for Church reform and unity with the Eastern Churches. His reconciliation of the pope with the German empire earned him a cardinal's hat under Pope Nicholas V.

Besides his work for the Church, Nicholas is known for his scholarship. He proposed that God is greater than even our highest knowledge (*docta ignorantia*), and that in God all apparent contradictions about God and his creation are resolved (*coincidentia oppositorum*). In his recognition of the limits of human reason, he is often considered a mystic, though because of his excellent critical scholarship he is a precursor of the Renaissance.

Nicholas' principal works include his call for Church reform, *On Catholic Concordance* (*De Concordantia Catholica*); *On Learned Ignorance* (*De Docta Ignorantia*); and *On the Vision of God* (*De Visione Dei*). He also recognized that the so-called *False Decretals* and the *Donation of Constantine* were forgeries, composed in the ninth century.

Norbert, St. (c. 1080–1134)

After a worldly early life, Norbert was dramatically converted in 1115 and very soon afterwards ordained a priest. He zealously sought to renew the other canons (diocesan officers) at Xanten, but when they opposed him he sold his possessions and went to Rome. There Pope Gelasius II gave him permission to preach wherever God led him.

Norbert preached in northern France, with miracles reportedly attending his sermons. At Prêmontre, he founded the Order of the Premonstratensians, dedicated to preaching and renewal, especially renewal of the clergy. Pope Honorius II approved his order in 1126 and appointed Norbert archbishop of Magdeburg, where he served as a zealous, reforming bishop until he stepped down shortly before his death in 1134. (Feast, June 6.)

Novatian (d. 257)

A priest of Rome in the third century, Novatian wrote a pioneering treatise on the Trinity—the first major theological work written in Latin. Sadly, he is more widely remembered today as the leader of a schismatic group and an "anti-pope" (someone claiming to be pope in opposition to the rightful holder of the office). After the great persecution of the emperor Decius (250–51), he strongly disagreed with Pope Cornelius' standards of readmission to the Church for those who had denied their faith ("lapsed" or apostasized) during the persecution. Novatian held that only God could forgive the sin of apostasy, though he was unclear and inconsistent in his position.

St. Cyprian* of Carthage supported Pope Cornelius' decision, and Novatian was excommunicated by a Roman synod in 251. Canon 8 of the Council of Nicea* (325) presented terms for the reconciliation of Novatian's followers with the Catholic Church.

O

Odoacer (c. 435–93)

A Germanic ruler of Italy, Odoacer is historically notable for deposing the last Roman emperor of the West, Romulus Augustus, in 476. He was an Arian* but was not actively involved in the affairs of the Church. He was defeated and killed in 493 by Theodoric, ruler of the Goths, who occupied Italy at the direction of the Eastern emperor Zeno.

Orange, Second Council of (529)

St. Caesarius of Arles* presided over this Gallic regional council. It defined more clearly the Catholic understanding of the absolute necessity of grace for salvation against the teachings of the semi-Pelagians, while at the same time excluding extreme interpretations of St. Augustine's* teaching that denied true human freedom in responding to grace. Although it is not an ecumenical council of the Catholic Church, the teaching of the Second Council of Orange was ratified by Pope Boniface II in 531.

Origen (c. 185–c. 254)

Origen is recognized as the greatest Christian scholar before the fourth century. The sixth chapter of Eusebius'* *History of the Church* is almost entirely devoted to this brilliant man's career. Eusebius reports that Origen grew up in a strong Christian home in Alexandria, Egypt, and his father, St. Leonidas, was martyred in 202 under the Roman emperor Septimus Severus. Origen longed to follow his father in martyrdom by turning himself in to the authorities, but his mother thwarted his plan by hiding his clothes.

A brilliant student, Origen studied philosophy and literature under Ammonius Saccas. Bishop Demetrius appointed the eighteen-year-old Origen head of the renowned catechetical school of Alexandria, where he served faithfully as a lay scholar for many years. When he was irregularly ordained a priest in Palestine in 230, Demetrius deprived him of his teaching post, and Origen took refuge in Caesarea, where he continued to teach and write. He died around 254 from tortures he suffered during the persecution of Decius.*

Origen has been denied the title of "saint" because some of his theological theories (for example, the preexistence of souls, that the devil will eventually be saved, the "lesser" divinity of the

Son when compared to the Father, and so on) were later declared heretical. However, during his lifetime he never knowingly taught anything contrary to the Catholic faith, and his views were highly regarded and profoundly shaped early Christian theology. His systematic theology is expressed most fully in *De Principiis* (*On First Principles*).

Origen was a radical ascetic Christian whose spiritual writings (such as *Exhortation to Martyrdom* and *On Prayer*) inspired and guided the then-emerging ascetic movement. His mysticism of progressive ascent to God through prayer, self-denial, and alms-giving is echoed and developed in many later mystical writings.

In biblical studies, Origen is known for his allegorical interpretation of Scripture, always seeking to determine the deeper, spiritual meaning of the sacred text. He wrote commentaries on almost every book of the Bible and produced the first work of multi-linear translation, the *Hexapla*. Altogether, according to St. Jerome,* Origen produced two thousand books, though most of them have been lost.

Otto I (912–73)

During a time of extreme social disorganization in Western Europe (rightly called the "Dark Ages"), this German ruler brought order and reestablished the Holy Roman Empire through his coronation by the corrupt Pope John XII in 962. Shortly thereafter, Otto deposed John and nominated his own candidate, who became Pope Leo VIII. Even though Otto I interfered in the affairs of the Church, he sought the unity of Church and state and fought corruption in the Church.

Our Lady of Guadalupe

Although she is not a historical figure in the ordinary sense, the appearances of Mary, the Mother of God, under this title have profoundly affected the history of the Western hemisphere. In 1531, a beautiful woman appeared to a native Mexican who had taken the Christian name Juan Diego when he had been converted to Catholicism by Franciscan priests in 1524 or 25. Mary asked Juan Diego to go to the bishop of Mexico City and request, on her behalf, that a shrine be built on the hill adjacent to where she had appeared to him.

The bishop was unconvinced, until one day Mary directed Juan Diego to mount the hill and to fill his *tilma* (cloak) with flowers (miraculously blooming out of season) to bring to the bishop as a sign. When Juan Diego did so, on his *tilma* was an image of Mary, appearing and clothed as a native Mexican princess who was expecting a child. So the shrine was built, and the *tilma* with its image of "Our Lady of Guadalupe" has been preserved to this day.

In the years immediately following Mary's appearances, an estimated more than six million native people of Mexico and surrounding tribes converted to Christianity due to this apparition. Our Lady of Guadalupe is the patroness of the Americas. (Feast, December 12.)

Pachomius, St. (c. 290–346)

Born in Egypt to pagan parents, Pachomius was converted by the witness of the charity of Christians while he was serving in the army in around 312. At his baptism he had a vision that led him to devote himself to ministry of service to others, which characterized his entire life. He became an ascetic (monk) living with Palamon, a holy hermit.

After Palamon's death, Pachomius continued this life of self-denial with his brother, John, but increasingly sensed the Lord's call to share the ascetic life by gathering monks to live in close proximity for common prayer and mutual support and service. His brother did not agree, but after John's death, Pachomius started the first community of ascetics at Tabennesi in the Egyptian desert. He also formulated a simple, gospel-based rule for the monks living in this community based on a covenant.

Pachomius soon founded other monasteries, including his headquarters at Phbow, and from there the idea of coenobitic monasticism (monks living in community with recognized authority and a rule of life) spread rapidly. Some settlements of monks numbered a thousand or more, and by the end of the fourth century the Pachomian communities in Egypt had an estimated seven thousand members. (Feast, May 9.)

Pallotti, St. Vincent (1795–1850)

A precursor of the "era of the laity," this Italian priest-theologian turned his primary attention to pastoral concerns and founded the Society of the Catholic Apostolate in 1835. Comprised of clergy and laity, the society's threefold mission was evangelization, deepening Catholics' spiritual life, and performing corporal and spiritual works of mercy. Vincent also had tremendous personal gifts of healing and preaching and was known for his generosity, often giving away his own clothes to the poor. He prayed fervently for the reunification of the separated Eastern churches with Rome. Worn out by his labors, he died at age fifty-five. (Feast, January 22.)

Pascal, Blaise (1623–62)

This profound French thinker of the seventeenth century may be studied as a scientist, as an austere Jansenist* Catholic, and as a Christian apologist. Pascal did groundbreaking work in geometry ("Pascal's triangle"), calculus, and the physics of air and liquids. In 1646 he became associated with the Jansenists of Port-Royal and defended the strict Jansenist morality against the perceived laxity of the Jesuits in his eighteen *Provincial Letters* (condemned in 1657 by the Congregation of the Index).

Pascal's spirituality is a fascinating blend of faith supported both by personal experience and by reason. On November 23, 1654, he had a profound experience of God ("the God of Abraham, the God of Isaac, the God of Jacob, and not of philosophers"), which he recorded in a "Memorial" that he carried with him for the rest of his life. He began writing a series of reflections (*Pensées*) on Christian faith in which he asserts the reality of original sin ("the greatness and wretchedness of man"), the need for a radical step of faith to accept Christ as Savior (a step ultimately made by "the heart" in that "the heart has its reasons of which reason knows not"), and (nonetheless) the reasonableness of faith as something that compels one to "wager" one's life and freedom on it, since one's eternal destiny hangs in the balance of that decision.

Pascal resisted both the growing tendency of his time to take a purely rationalistic approach to Christianity leading to deism, and the pure fideism ("faith alone") of Protestantism, which rejected reasoned arguments or demonstrations of the truth of Christian faith. Pascal died in 1662 at only forty years of age. It is a tragedy for the Catholic Church in France that no one of his intellectual stature emerged in later years in France to refute the powerful influence of rationalistic deism and religious skepticism that dominated French intellectual circles in the eighteenth century.

Patrick, St. (c. 390–c. 460)

Born into a Christian home near the Western shores of Britain in the early fourth century, Patrick (also known as "Sucat") was raised there until he was taken captive by raiders and brought as a slave to present-day Ireland. He tended the sheep of a chieftain named Miliucc in Northern Ireland (Slemish in County Antrim). In captivity, he prayed and fasted, and a vision directed him to escape to a ship.

After journeying to Gaul and Italy, Patrick finally returned to his family in Britain. He studied for ordination in Wales and possibly in Auxere, France—longing to return to Ireland as a missionary. Others, such as Palladius, had tried and failed to convert Ireland, but in 432, at age forty, Patrick returned and soon converted

Dichu, a local chieftain.

From there, Patrick decided that on Easter morning he would approach the high king Laoghaire at Tara and preach the gospel. There, Patrick defeated the Druid magicians. The high king, though not converted, allowed Patrick to preach throughout the land. The number of his converts grew steadily, as he brought the light of the gospel into pagan darkness.

Patrick's preaching was direct and clear, and he used simple devices to teach, such as the shamrock to explain the Blessed Trinity. Wherever he went, he sought permission from the local chieftains to build a church. By the end of his life, hundreds had been built, and Patrick had ordained more than 3,000 priests and consecrated 370 bishops. The surviving writings of this "Apostle of Ireland" include a letter to a British chieftain Coroticus, as well as his *Confession*, defending his character and ministry against criticism. (Feast, March 17.)

Paul III, Pope (1468–1549)

Overcoming a sinful early life, after he was ordained to the priesthood Alesandro Farnese reformed himself and became the first great pope (1534–49) of the Catholic Reformation. He appointed gifted men— Reginald Pole, Gasparo Contarini,* G. Murone, and G. P. Caraffa (the future Pope Paul IV)—to the College of Cardinals and encouraged the new or reformed religious orders, especially the Jesuits, whose rule he approved in 1540. Paul III also re-established the Inquisition* as the "Holy Office" to fight heresy in the Church and succeeded in convening the great reform Council at Trent* in 1545.

As a Renaissance pope, Paul patronized the arts, enlisting Michelangelo* to finish *The Last Judgment* in the Sistine chapel and continuing the building of St. Peter's Basilica in Rome. Though he failed to bring Henry VIII* and other Protestant rulers back to the Catholic Church, his reform efforts within the Church produced significant and lasting results.

Paul VI, Pope (1897–1978)

Giovanni Battista Montini, ordained in 1920, was a teacher and a diplomat, serving in the papal administration until being named bishop of Milan in 1951 by Pope Pius XII.* He had declined the cardinal's hat offered by Pius, but was one of the first to be named cardinal by Pope John XXIII,* who called on him to take a leading role in the Second Vatican* Council. It was not surprising that Montini was elected pope upon John's death in 1963.

Taking the name Paul VI, he continued the council in the style of John XXIII, trusting in the Holy Spirit to guide the bishops in their discussions and decrees. After the council ended in 1965, it was Paul's challenging task to guide its proper implementation. Many observers find it remarkable that Paul directed the massive conciliar reforms without a major schism developing.

Paul carried out the council's teaching by his conciliatory meetings with leaders of other churches and religions, such as his visits to Greek Patriarch Athenagoras I, in which the mutual excommunications of 1054 were lifted. Paul VI was a "pilgrim pope," spreading the message of Christ personally to many nations, according to the example of his namesake, St. Paul. His *Credo of the People of God* was an important contemporary expression of the faith.

Paul's encyclical letter on social development, *Populorium Progressio* (1967), continued the tradition of Catholic social teaching begun by Pope Leo XIII.* However, his last encyclical letter, *Humanae Vitae* (1968), repeating the Church's consistent teaching against artificial contraception, caused tremendous controversy, especially within the Western Church. In the later years of his papacy, Paul seemed increasingly burdened by the outcry against *Humanae Vitae*, the difficulties in proper implementation of the Second Vatican Council, and the world crises in Vietnam, the Middle East, and the Cold War. His hope and solace rested in the powerful movements of evangelization and renewal that were set afoot by the Council, such as the gathering of ten thousand charismatic Catholics in Rome in 1975. This "Pope of the Holy Spirit" died of a heart attack in 1978.

Pelagianism

Pelagius, a British monk who traveled to Rome around 405, taught that God's grace was helpful but not necessary for human salvation. He also denied that original sin intrinsically corrupted human nature, viewing the sin of Adam and Eve instead as a bad example that led people into habits of sin. These sinful patterns, however, could be overcome by free will, guided by an informed intellect and a well-formed conscience. He encouraged a moral renewal in Rome, especially directed to upper-class Christians, whom Pelagius urged to become models of virtue for their fellow citizens.

Pelagius' views were opposed by St. Jerome* in the East (where Pelagius moved in 412) and by St. Augustine,* the "Doctor of Grace," in the Latin West. Augustine's own experience was that his free will and desire to do good were totally powerless to deliver him from the bondage of sin. Only God's free gift of grace could do this, reversing and healing the crippling effects of original sin.

"Pelagianism" was condemned as heresy by a synod at Carthage in 418, by Pope Zosimus following that synod, and by the ecumenical Council of Ephesus in 431. But among many Christians down to our own time, Pelagian tendencies continue. Beginning with the correct assumption that human nature is basically good, they mistakenly deny or underestimate the effects of original sin, concluding that through good intentions, proper education, and sufficient moral effort human beings are capable of being and doing good apart from any particular grace of God. This belief is essentially the Pelagian heresy.

Pepin (Pippin) III (714–68)

In 741, Pepin, the son of Charles Martel,* succeeded him as effective ruler of the kingdom of the Franks. Pope Zacharias called for Pepin to be anointed as king in 751, officially ending the Merovingian dynasty begun by Clovis.* When Zacharias' successor, Pope Stephen II, crossed the Alps to beg Pepin to defend Rome against the Lombards, Pepin agreed, and Stephen anointed the king and his sons, declaring Pepin "patrician of the Romans."

Pepin in turn gave the pope a document, the *Donation of Pepin*, which declared Rome and a number of neighboring cities and territories to be possessions of the pope. Through this action, the Papal States were born. The king made good on his promise to defend the pope by defeating the Lombards in 754 and 756.

Pepin also fostered the reform of the Frankish church begun by St. Boniface* and instituted the Roman liturgical rite in his territories instead of the Gallican rite. He died in 768 and was succeeded by his son, Charlemagne.*

Perpetua, St. and Felicity, St. (d. 203)

These two heroic women were among many martyred in Carthage, North Africa, in 203. Perpetua was a married noblewoman with a newborn son, who courageously accepted martyrdom along with other members of her household, including her slave, St. Felicity. Before her martyrdom, Felicity said to the guards in reference to her death: "Another will be with me, who will suffer for me, because I will suffer for him." (Feast, March 7.)

Peter Lombard (c. 1100–60)

Born in Lombardy, Peter emerged as one of the most influential teachers in the Church of the twelfth century. His greatest work was the *Book of Sentences*, in which he sets forth the teaching of many Latin and Greek fathers of the early Church in an orderly arrangement. This work became the standard theological textbook in the Middle Ages, surpassed only by the *Summa Theologica* of St. Thomas Aquinas.*

Peter was one of the first to specify that there are seven sacraments and to identify the Holy Spirit as Charity or Love. He spent most of his life as a teacher but was named archbishop of Paris shortly before his death in 1160.

Photius (c. 810–c. 895)

Photius was at the center of a storm of controversy in the ninth century over Church office and authority. After the Byzantine Emperor Michael III deposed Ignatius as patriarch of Constantinople, the scholarly monk Photius (still a layman) was appointed to succeed him. Pope Nicholas I* denounced this action and declared the appointment of Photius invalid. This unilateral declaration of the pope about Eastern affairs offended the Byzantines and led them to excommunicate Nicholas at a council in 667.

However, a new Byzantine emperor,

Basil, reversed this decision and expelled Photius. This act was confirmed by the eighth ecumenical council (recognized only by the Catholic Church), the Third Council of Constantinople* (869–70). Thus, the temporary schism of East and West was healed, but important issues remained unresolved, especially the question of the authority of the pope.

Ironically, when the reinstated Patriarch Ignatius died in 877, Photius was once again appointed patriarch of Constantinople by the Byzantine emperor. This time the Church in the West supported Photius' appointment. Photius served in this position until 886. He resigned when Leo VI became Byzantine emperor, and little more is known of his life.

Pius VII, Pope (1740–1823)

The papacy of Pope Pius VII (1800–1823) was a turning point for the papacy in modern times. Taking over after the previous pope (Pius VI) had been driven from Rome by the French Directory, he had to deal with the powerful new French emperor, Napoleon Bonaparte. Pius appointed a brilliant statesman, Ercole Consalvi, to be his cardinal secretary of state, and Consalvi negotiated the Concordat of 1801 with Napoleon.

Napoleon, however, added his own

"Organic Articles" in 1802, which tightened his control over the Catholic Church in France. Pius made a bold move by going to Paris in 1804 to crown Napoleon emperor, hoping to wrest some concessions from him in person. But Napoleon's act of crowning himself and his queen symbolized his view of the pope's rightful place.

When Napoleon began his war of conquest, he expected Pius' support. Instead, the pope declared neutrality, prompting Napoleon to occupy Rome in 1808 and annex the Papal States in 1809. When the pope excommunicated Napoleon and all who participated in the annexation, Pius was arrested, removed from Rome, and isolated from his advisors.

Year after year, Pius refused to cooperate with Napoleon, and his stature grew in the eyes of the world. When Napoleon fell in 1814, Pius returned triumphantly to Rome, and his secretary, Consalvi, negotiated the return of the Papal States at the Congress of Vienna (1814–15). The pope vigorously set about restoring the Catholic Church throughout Europe, and reinstituted the Society of Jesus in 1814, which had been suppressed by Clement XIV* in 1773.

Pius was also a patron of learning and the arts, while at the same time opposing atheism and indifferentism.

His example of prayer and faith in outlasting the attacks on the Church by the French Revolution and Napoleon restored the influence and prestige of the papacy, which had been tarnished in the eighteenth century.

Pius IX, Blessed Pope (1792–1878)

Having the longest papacy in history (1846–78), Blessed Pope Pius IX lived in a time of tremendous social and intellectual upheaval. Son of an Italian count, Giovanni Maria Mastai-Feretti was thought to be a "liberal" churchman, which at the time meant being open to social change and experiments in democratic and representative government. When elected pope in 1846, he appeared to fulfill this reputation by supporting the movement for Italian unity ("*Risorgimento*") and seeking political reforms in the Papal States.

However, when Pius refused to support a war against Austria, rebels turned against him, murdering his prime minister and forcing him to flee. After the French army restored Pius to Rome in 1849, he understandably rejected liberal social policies. Pius' political power and influence declined as the Papal States were taken over one by one. Victor Emmanuel's conquest of Rome in 1870 completed the pope's loss of temporal power, which was never to be restored.

In this situation, Pius focused on the spiritual authority and leadership of the papacy. He established new dioceses and missions and revived the Church's hierarchy in England (1850) and the Netherlands (1853). While the pope's temporal power waned, he was vigorous in clarifying doctrine.

Pius defined the dogma of Mary's immaculate conception in 1854 and authored the *Syllabus of Errors* and the accompanying encyclical letter *Quanta cura* in 1864, which condemned errors he perceived arising in the Church stemming from "progress, liberalism, and modern civilization." Many observers saw some of Pius' statements as reactionary, attacking everything "modern." In his own mind, he simply was defending and clarifying traditional Catholic doctrine, which was being questioned.

With his warm and winning personality, Pius sought to affirm the spiritual and moral authority of the papacy. The climax of this effort was his calling of the First Vatican Council (1869–70), which formally defined papal primacy and infallibility in *Pastor Aeternus* and affirmed the unity of faith and reason in *Dei Filius* (though stressing the necessity and primacy of faith). The Ultramontane movement of this time emphasized the office of the pope as a sure anchor of truth and guidance in a changing world.

Because the First Vatican Council was cut short by the outbreak of the Franco-Prussian War, its agenda of addressing other issues (such as the role of the bishops and the laity) were never completed. As a result, Pius is remembered primarily as the pope who confronted the errors of the modern world and who established the pope as the Catholic Church's primary moral and spiritual guide in this world.

Pius X, Pope St. (1835–1914)

Guiseppe Sarto (pope 1903–14) was the last pontiff to be declared a saint and the first since St. Pius V (pope 1566–72) was canonized in 1712. Pius X was canonized, of course, for his personal holiness, which was evidenced by his deep love of Christ in the Eucharist and in the liturgy, and by his pure-hearted efforts to renew the Church. His renewal efforts began when he brought new life to the indifferent diocese of Mantua as its bishop (1884–93). Because of this success, Sarto was raised to the cardinalate by Pope Leo XIII* and made patriarch of Venice, where he served with distinction and energy.

Upon his election as pope in 1903 he chose the motto "To restore all things in Christ." He confronted anti-

Catholic governments in France and Portugal, which finally led to the total separation of Church and state in these countries.

Pius is best known for two things: his liturgical/Eucharistic renewal and his condemnation of the "modernist" heresy. He worked for the renewal of the liturgy (including the restoration of Gregorian chant) and encouraged frequent (even daily) reception of Holy Communion, lowering the normal age of First Communion to seven. He condemned a collection of modern errors, many of them false approaches to interpreting Scripture, which he labeled "modernism."

Pius listed and condemned these errors in *Lamentabili Sane* and *Pascendi Dominici Gregis* (both 1907) and required the clergy to take an oath against modernism (1910). While some have viewed this policy as a "witch hunt" and repressive of critical scholarship, Pius' anti-modernism did preserve the unity of the faith and compelled priests and scholars to evaluate carefully their methods and teachings. He also called for a revised breviary and a revision of the code of canon law, reorganized the Roman Curia, and established "Catholic Action" as an authorized form of Catholic social ministry.

In spite of his concern for maintain-

ing peace in Europe, World War I began during his reign, and this saintly pope, deeply saddened by this tragedy, died only a few days after its outbreak. Pius was canonized in 1954. (Feast, August 21.)

Pius XI, Pope (1857–1939)

Achille Ratti was a scholarly pope (a prefect of the Vatican Library) who had also distinguished himself as nuncio to Poland, remaining in Warsaw during the Bolshevik invasion of 1920. The following year he was made a cardinal archbishop of Milan, and the year after that he was elected pope. He negotiated the Lateran Treaty of 1929 with Benito Mussolini, creating the modern Vatican City State.

In 1937 he issued encyclicals condemning communism (*Divini Redem-ptoris*) and Nazi policies (*Mit Brennender Sorge*, "With Burning Sorrow"). The latter was written in German so it could be read from every Catholic pulpit in Germany.

Pius was an active pope who promoted missionary work (the number of missionaries doubled in his reign), Catholic Action, traditional Catholic marriage (*Casti Connubii*, 1930), and Catholic social teaching and involvement in social issues (*Quadragesimo Anno*, 1931). He established the feast of Christ the King in 1925 to counter secularism and declare Jesus the King and Lord of this world. He also canonized many saints who were active in the world, such as St. Thomas More,* St. John Bosco,* and St. Thérèse de Lisieux* (with her passion for the missions). In spite of his efforts to foster world peace, Pius was burdened by persecution of the Church in Mexico, the Spanish Civil War, and the beginning of the Second World War. He died suddenly from illness in 1939.

Pius XII, Pope (1876–1958)

A member of a respected Roman family, Eugenio Pacelli had extensive diplomatic experience that made him an ideal candidate for the papacy at the dark beginning of the Second World War in 1939. He was a pope of peace who succeeded in keeping Rome an open (free) city by maintaining the strict neutrality of the Vatican called for by the Lateran Treaty of 1929. This enabled the Vatican to administer relief to countless war victims and to offer asylum to hundreds of refugees, including Jewish refugees.

Pius has been denounced for this neutrality and for failure to speak out more strongly against Hitler. In response to these criticisms, his defenders point to Pius' many clear denunciations of racial extermination and his practical aid extended to great numbers of Jews (praised by the chief Rabbi of Rome, Dr. Israel Zolli, after the war).

Pius published a number of encyclical letters that began to reverse the defensive posture of the papacy toward modern thought and scholarship. They prepared the way for the Second Vatican* Council called for by his successor, Pope John XXIII.* These encyclicals include *Mystici corporis Christi* (1943, presenting the Church in more spiritual and less institutional terms); *Divino afflante Spiritu* (1943, authorizing limited use of modern biblical criticism); *Mediator Dei* (1947, on the renewal of the liturgy, advocating lay participation); and in a more traditional vein, *Humani generis* (1950, warning against certain intellectual trends) and the definition of Mary's assumption into heaven (1950, *Munificentissimus Deus*).

Pius also increased and internationalized the number of cardinals, reducing the number of Italian cardinals to one third. He died, after frequent illnesses, in 1958.

Polycarp of Smyrna, St. (c. 69–c. 155)

One of the most honored bishops in the early Church, Polycarp was a disciple of the apostle* John himself and instructed the great theologian-bishop

Irenaeus of Lyons.* Though not as original in his thought as his contemporary, St. Ignatius of Antioch,* Polycarp faithfully passed on the Church's doctrine and called his flock to holiness by word and example. We see these concerns reflected in Polycarp's letter to the Philippians, in St. Ignatius' letter to Polycarp, and in the extraordinary account of Polycarp's martyrdom, which occurred in 155 during the rule of Aurelius Caesar.

The *Martyrdom of Polycarp* accentuates details parallel to Jesus' passion and death, emphasizing the martyr's death as a sacrifice of thanksgiving (that is, a Eucharistic sacrifice). Polycarp's commitment to Jesus resounded in his words to the Roman official trying to convince him to save his own life by denying his faith. The aged bishop exclaimed: "Eighty-six years I have served him, and he never did me any wrong. How can I now blaspheme my king and God?" (Feast, February 23.)

Quietism

A term often used to designate any system of spirituality that minimizes human activity and responsibility, Quietism refers more specifically to the teaching of several seventeenth-century spiritual writers, especially Miguel de Molinos,* Madame Guyon,* and Archbishop François Fénelon.* The essential principle of Quietism is its condemnation of all human effort. It teaches that in order to be perfect, human beings must attain complete passivity and annihilation of will, to such an extent that they care neither for heaven nor hell, nor for their own salvation. These and related teachings were condemned by Pope Innocent XI in his bull *Coelestis Pastor* in 1687.

R

Radewyns, Florentius (1350–1400)
Radewyns, a Dutchman, succeeded Gerhard Groote,* who founded the lay renewal community called the Brethren of the Common Life.* Radewyns founded a famous center of the Brethren at Deventer and was also a teacher of Thomas á Kempis,* author of *The Imitation of Christ*.

Rahner, Karl (1904–84)
Rahner was a German Jesuit whose theology and work as a *peritus* (expert) at the Second Vatican Council* significantly influenced the twentieth-century Church. Formed as a scholar by Jesuit Joseph Maréchal and by existential philosopher Martin Heidegger, Rahner spearheaded a new approach to theology known as "transcendental Thomism." His major writings include *Sacramentum Mundi* (1968–1970), *Spirit in the World* (revised 1957), *Hearers of the Word* (1941), and a multi-volume collection of essays, *Theological Investigations*. After a lengthy and fruitful teaching career at the University of Munich and Münster, Rahner died in 1984 at age eighty.

Raphael (Raffaele Sanzio) (1483–1520)
Celebrated as the most famous Renaissance painter, Raphael's great work began with *The Crucifixion* in 1502 and included many famous Madonnas. In 1508, Pope Julius II enlisted him to paint at the Vatican and in St. Peter's Basilica; his works there include the *Disputa*, *St. Peter Released from Prison*, and many biblical scenes on the ceiling. Pope Leo X* appointed him chief architect of St. Peter's in 1514. He died in 1520 while still working on *The Transfiguration*, which was completed by his students and is displayed in the Vatican.

Ratzinger, Joseph (1927–)
A German theologian, Ratzinger taught at the universities of Bonn, Münster, Tübingen, and Regensburg until, in 1977, he was made a cardinal and archbishop of Münich by Pope Paul VI.* He was known as a progressive theologian and helped found the forward-looking theological series, *Concilium*. Recognized for his fidelity to the Church and her tradition, Ratzinger was appointed Prefect of the Sacred Congregation for the Doctrine of the Faith in 1981 by Pope John

Paul II* and has remained in that post as one of John Paul's closest advisors.

Robert de Nobili, S.J. (1577–1656)
One of the most successful Jesuit missionaries of the early seventeenth century, this Italian priest arrived in India in 1604 and assumed the lifestyle and dress of an Indian Brahman ascetic. Despite the success of his methods (de Nobili is said to have converted up to a hundred thousand Indians), many in the Church opposed his approach. Controversy swirled until Pope Gregory XV approved this early form of "inculturation" in 1623. De Nobili also authored works explaining Catholic faith and theology in Sanskrit, Tamil, and Telugu, as well as Latin, Italian, and Portuguese.

Robert of Molesme, St.
(c. 1027–1111)
Famous for founding the monastery of Cîteaux—and the Cistercian order—St. Robert devoted his life to monastic renewal. His first notable success was the founding of a monastery for some hermits at Molesme (in Burgundy) in 1075. After Molesme declined in fervor, he went to Cîteaux in 1098, whose members were called Cistercians.

The strict Cistercian renewal and spirit spread to other monasteries.

Robert took it back to Molesme, where he returned as abbot until his death, and St. Bernard,* perhaps the most famous Cistercian, brought it from Cîteaux to his new monastery at Clairvaux. Thus the Cistercian reform became a significant instrument of reform and renewal of monastic life in the eleventh and twelfth centuries. (Feast, April 29.)

Romero, Oscar (1917–80)
Ordained a priest in 1942, Romero was made bishop of Santiago de Maria, El Salvador, in 1972, and archbishop of San Salvador in 1977. He took a strong stand for social justice and opposed government oppression of the poor, leading to his nomination for the Nobel Peace Prize. He was assassinated on March 24, 1980, as he was saying Mass in a small chapel adjoining his quarters.

Romuald, St. (c. 950–1027)
Romuald contributed to the ascetic renewal of the early eleventh century by founding a number of austere monasteries and hermitages in Italy. He sought to live a life of extreme penance and prayer beginning at age twenty, when he witnessed his father, a nobleman, kill another man in a duel. The center of his movement was at Campus Maduli, from which the her-

mitages and monasteries he founded received the name "Camaldolese." St. Peter Damian* wrote Romuald's biography. (Feast, June 19.)

Rose of Lima, St. (1586–1617)

Born in Lima, Peru, in 1586 with the baptismal name Isabel, in 1597 she took "Rosc" as her confirmation name. Even in her youth at home she practiced severe self-mortification and devoted herself to prayer, following the example of St. Catherine of Siena.* Like Catherine, she lived at home and, in spite of her family's misunderstanding and insistence that she marry, became a Third Order Dominican* and devoted herself to prayer of reparation for the social sins she saw inflicted on the native peoples.

Rose also cared for the sick, the elderly, and homeless children. After much physical suffering (some say due to the severity of her penances), she died in 1617 at age thirty-one, and in 1671 became the first native of the Americas to be canonized, by Pope Clement X. She is honored as patroness of South America and of the Philippines. (Feast, August 23.)

Savanarola, Girolamo (1452-1498)
This radical religious reformer joined the Dominican* order in 1474. Adopting a rigorous ascetic life, Savanarola came to prominence in Florence, Italy, where he preached sermons against the decadence and immorality of Renaissance life there. He prophesied the downfall of the powerful Medici family, which occurred when King Charles VIII of France took over the city and followed many of Savanarola's political ideas.

Savanarola continued to act and preach against public immorality and abuses in the Church, even criticizing the Roman curia and Pope Alexander VI. The pope ordered Savanarola to cease preaching, then excommunicated him in 1497 when he refused to obey. Eventually, Savanarola was arrested, imprisoned, and hanged in 1498. Though he left behind a legacy of reform and some powerful apologetic works (such as *The Triumph of the Cross*), some of his sermons were placed on the Index of Forbidden books. Protestant reformers later (though falsely) considered him a forerunner of the Reformation.

Scholastica, St. (c. 480–c. 543)
The sister of St. Benedict of Nursia,* this holy woman led a convent of women to live according to Benedict's *Rule*, beginning a great tradition of Western monasticism for women religious. (Feast, February 10.)

Seton, St. Elizabeth Ann (1774–1821)
The first American-born saint, Elizabeth Bayley was raised an Anglican in New York City. She married William Seton in 1794 and first encountered Catholics in Italy, where her husband died of an illness in 1803. There, the Filichi family took her in, and she experienced the presence of Jesus in them and in her prayers before the Blessed Sacrament.

This profound event led Seton to receive instruction and become a Catholic back in America in 1805. To support her children, she opened a boarding school in New York, but when her sister-in-law, Cecilia Seton, was influenced by Elizabeth to become a Catholic, strong opposition mounted. Religious toleration was an ideal not yet realized in America.

Seton first thought of entering a convent in Canada, but Archbishop

John Carroll* of Baltimore convinced her to come to his diocese, where she opened a school in 1808. When other young Catholic women joined her, the bishop asked her to take over a boarding school for poor children in Emmitsburg, Maryland. She did this and eventually started a branch of the Sisters of Charity that was approved by Archbishop Carroll in 1812.

The religious community spread to other cities, with Mother Seton as its superior. Her work continued until her death in 1821. She was canonized by Pope Paul VI* in 1975. (Feast, January 4.)

Segneri, Paul (1624–94)

A seventeenth-century Italian Jesuit who was hailed as the greatest preacher in Italy, Segneri followed in the footsteps of St. Bernadine of Siena* and Savonarola.* His Lenten retreats formed the basis of the highly successful Catholic renewal method known as the parish mission, which spread throughout Europe and eventually to the United States in the nineteenth century.

Serra, Blessed Junípero (1713–84)

Born Miguel Serra in Majorca, Spain, Fr. Junípero Serra, O.F.M, was the founder of the California missions. Before becoming a missionary, he earned a doctorate in theology and taught for seven years at the University of Majorca. In 1749 his wish to do missionary work began to be fulfilled when he was sent to "New Spain" (Mexico).

Serra's first assignment was among the Pame tribe, and after nine years every person in the region professed and practiced the Catholic faith. He hoped to go north to bring the gospel to new territories, but was assigned, for eight years, to preach missions and retreats across Mexico. Finally, at age fifty-five, with asthma and ulcerated legs and feet, he was appointed president of the missions in Baja California, which the Franciscans took over when the Jesuits were expelled from Spanish dominions in 1767.

Over the next fifteen years (1769–84), Serra founded nine new missions, including San Diego, San Gabriel, San Luis Obispo, San Francisco, San Juan Capistrano, and Santa Clara. He had traveled more than six thousand miles on foot in the previous twenty years. In the first six months of visiting the Baja California missions, he walked another thousand miles before beginning his new foundations in Alta (upper) California.

The missions in present-day California were almost never begun. At what was to be his first mission, San

Diego, Serra arrived to find that scurvy had killed the crew of the supply ship, and only a few weakened soldiers remained alive. The native people, seeing their condition, became bolder and more hostile. The mission would have had to be abandoned at the end of Serra's nine-day novena to St. Joseph, but on the ninth day a supply ship arrived, and the first mission was established.

Serra's zeal for the conversion of the native people drove him on, undeterred by the frequent attacks of hostile tribes. He was constant in prayer and preaching, which resulted in mass conversions—an estimated 6,700 baptisms in the missions he founded by the time of his death in 1784. As an administrator of missions he was meticulous in keeping track of and using every resource (human and material) given to him to advance the cause of Christ.

Serra died at his northernmost mission of St. Carlos in Monterey at age seventy. He was beatified by Pope John Paul II* in 1988.

Sheen, Fulton J. (1895–1979)

An American, ordained in 1919, Sheen spent the years before 1950 as a scholar and teacher at Catholic University of America, and after 1950 (as a bishop) as one of the Catholic Church's greatest preachers and media figures. He is remembered especially for his popular ABC television series on the Catholic Faith (*Life is Worth Living*) and the more than sixty books he published.

Simeon the Stylite, St. (c. 390–459)

Simeon was the product of a Syriac Christianity that was already very austere. He lived in a community of monks for about ten years before he was expelled. Then he went to live alone, first in a domed hut atop a hill, and then on the top of three successively higher pillars, where he spent his life in prayer and penance, exposed to the elements.

Pilgrims and people seeking advice flocked to him. Healings were sometimes reported, and Simeon's fame eventually reached from Britain to the Persian Empire. A few hardy disciples (such as Daniel the Stylite) imitated him, but for most, Simeon remained a model of one radical response to the gospel. He died in 459, more than seventy years old. (Feast, January 5.)

Soubirous, St. Bernadette (1844–79)

Bernadette was declared a saint by Pope Pius XI* in 1933 because of her humility, faith, and constancy in the great suffering she endured from illness, which led to her death at age thirty-five. However, she will always be remembered as the young peasant girl to whom the Blessed Virgin Mary appeared in a series of eighteen visitations beginning on February 11, 1858.

"Our Lady of Lourdes" revealed herself to Bernadette as "the Immaculate Conception." That theological truth had been defined as dogma by Pope Pius IX only four years earlier and was unknown to Bernadette. The Blessed Virgin Mary also asked Bernadette to have a chapel built near a spring as a pilgrimage site. Seeing no spring, Bernadette followed the Lady's instructions to dig in the ground. A tiny trickle of muddy water appeared, which became a small stream that has since produced hundreds of documented cases of healings through Mary's intercession.

When the visitations ceased after a couple of months, Bernadette was subjected to a mixture of scrutiny, criticism, and adulation. She retreated to the care of the Sisters of Charity at Nevers and joined the order in 1866 as Sr. Marie Bernarde. Living there, as she desired, in simplicity and obscurity, she found that her childhood asthma worsened, and she suffered greatly from tuberculosis of the bone before her early death. (Feast, April 16.)

Spellman, Francis Joseph (1889–1967)

An American Catholic, made archbishop of New York in 1939 and cardinal in 1946, Spellman was the most influential American Catholic in both the Catholic Church and in American politics of his time. As a friend of Pope Pius XII,* he was an important link between the Vatican and the Roosevelt administration during World War II, in which the Vatican remained neutral. He promoted the work of Jesuit John Courtney Murray* in the Vatican *Declaration on Religious Freedom* (*Dignitatis Humanae*).

In America, Spellman defended Catholic rights and participation in society, and he stood up against immorality in media and artificial contraception. He was fluent in several languages, which he used as both a diplomat and a translator.

Stein, St. Edith (1891–1942)

Edith Stein (Teresa Benedicta of the Cross) was raised in a devout Jewish family in Breslau, Germany. She did not share her family's faith, however, but became an atheist by age thirteen. A precocious student at the University of Göttingen, she was attracted by the phenomenological school of philosopher Edmund Husserl. She became Husserl's assistant at the University of

Freiburg until she earned her doctorate there in 1916.

Stein's reading of St. Teresa of Avila's* autobiography eventually led her to be baptized in the Catholic Church in 1922 and to join the Carmelites at Cologne in 1934. Being smuggled out of Germany into the Netherlands in 1938 did not save her from the murderous anti-Semitic policies of the Nazis. She was arrested during the Nazi occupation of the Netherlands and taken to Auschwitz, where she died in the gas chamber. Though her philosophical writings were brilliant, it was her profound understanding and imitation of Christ's suffering—the cross—that led Pope John Paul II* to canonize her in 1998. She was also declared a copatroness of Europe. (Feast, August 10.)

Stephen of Hungary, St. (975–1038)

The first king of Hungary was also responsible for the conversion of the Magyar people to the Catholic faith. At age ten (c. 985), Stephen was baptized with his father, Geza, possibly by St. Adalbert of Prague, a Czech martyr-bishop who converted and baptized many Hungarians and Prussians. Stephen succeeded his father as ruler of Hungary in 997 and was zealous for the spread of the Catholic faith, bap-tizing all whom he conquered.

Loyal to the pope, he was crowned by Pope Sylvester II in 1000. When his wife bore him no male heir, he dedicated Hungary to Mary as its queen and sovereign ruler. (Feast, August 16.)

Suenens, Leon-Josef (1904–96)

One of the most influential prelates of the Second Vatican Council,* Suenens was vice-rector of the University of Louvain (1940–45) and archbishop and primate of Belgium (1961–79). He was made a cardinal in 1962 and served as a moderator of the Second Vatican Council*. Suenens proposed that the council should have a document specifically on the Church's role in the modern world (which became *Gaudium et Spes*) and that gifts of the Holy Spirit (*charismata*) should be included in the *Dogmatic Constitution on the Church* (*Lumen Gentium*) as an essential part of the Church's nature.

Suenens wrote extensively on the renewal of religious life (*The Nun in the Modern World*) and on the important role of laity in the Church (*Coresponsibility in the Church*, 1968). He was also the highest-ranking churchman to promote the charismatic renewal movement in the Catholic Church and fostered its acceptance and growth worldwide, as seen in his book *A New Pentecost?* (1974).

Suso, Blessed Henry
(c. 1295–1366)

Suso was a German Dominican mystic who studied under Meister Eckhart* in Cologne (1322–1325). He defended Eckhart after the latter's teachings were condemned in 1329, which led Suso to be censured by his order and deprived of his university teaching position. However, he continued to travel, preach, and act as a spiritual advisor in Switzerland and the upper Rhine area. His work *The Little Book of Eternal Wisdom* was one of the most popular devotional works of the late Middle Ages. Suso was beatified by Pope Gregory XVI in 1831.

Tatian (second century)

A native of Syria, Tatian studied under St. Justin Martyr* in Rome, but proved to be much more austere and narrow-minded. His one surviving work, *Discourse to the Greeks*, recognizes no value in Greek philosophy and civilization; Christianity is for him the sole divine source of truth and wisdom.

As a strict ascetic following the tenets of an early movement called Encratism, he rejected marriage and procreation as evil, and hence was expelled from the Church. Returning to Syria in the late second century, he composed the first synthesis or "harmony" of the four Gospels, the *Diatessaron*, which is mentioned by historians of the time but has since been lost.

Tauler, John (1300–61)

A German Dominican preacher, Tauler was one of the "Rhineland mystics" who was influenced by the work of Meister Eckhart.* Tauler spent his climactic years in Strasbourg, where he preached, directed nuns, and cared for the sick, especially during the "Black Death" of 1348. His spirituality balanced the inward contemplation of God and the practice of the virtues.

Tauler also was influenced by St. Thomas Aquinas'* teaching on the vision of God, though he departed from Aquinas on some points. He is known for his reflections on the nature of suffering, which had an impact on German piety. His thought, though perfectly orthodox, later influenced Martin Luther* as well.

Teilhard de Chardin, Pierre (1881–1955)

Teilhard was a twentieth-century French Jesuit theologian and scientist who sought to bring theology and science together in an innovative way. He adapted the evolutionary theory to produce a view of creation and spirit evolving toward a final point (the "omega point"), which would be the fullness of Christ who is "the Alpha and the Omega" (see Rv 21:6). The Catholic Church silenced Teilhard for a time and has warned against possible misunderstanding of his works. Nonetheless, his major works—*The Diving Milieu* (1957) and *The Phenomenon of Man* (1955)—have opened the way for further exploration of the synthesis of Church teaching, theology, and science.

Tekakwitha, Blessed Kateri (c. 1656–80)

The "Lily of the Mohawks," Kateri was the daughter of a Mohawk chieftain and a Christian mother living near present-day Auriesville, New York. She was orphaned by a smallpox epidemic at age four, which also left her scarred and partially blind. As a chieftain's daughter, she was a desirable bride, but she dismayed her uncle and her tribe by refusing to marry.

Kateri was baptized on Easter, 1676, which created such opposition in her tribe that she was taken to a Jesuit Indian mission near Montreal, Canada. There she spent three years of intense prayer and penance, exhibiting deep union with God, before her death of illness in 1680. On her deathbed, the scars of her smallpox disappeared, leaving her face unblemished. Soon afterwards, miracles were reported through her intercession. She was beatified by Pope John Paul II* in 1980. (Feast, July 14.)

Teresa of Avila, St. (1515–82)

One of the greatest mystics and reformers in Catholic history, Teresa was the first woman to be declared a Doctor of the Church, in 1970. She was one of twelve children, born in Avila, Spain. A devout child, she not surprisingly joined a Carmelite con-

vent in Avila at age twenty, in 1535.

In spite of continual poor health, she persevered in her vocation, though the laxity of her convent's rules did not call her on to radical holiness. That path began in 1555, after twenty years as a Carmelite, when she was deeply moved while praying before a statue of Christ's scourging and gave herself up entirely to him. Thereafter, the Lord blessed Teresa with many spiritual favors, which she revealed (under obedience), in her autobiography. Her spiritual directors, St. Peter of Alcántara, St. Francis Borgia, and Dominic Bañez, provided valuable guidance.

As her own spiritual life intensified, Teresa began to thirst for the renewal of her Carmelite Order. In the face of rigorous opposition, she opened a reformed ("discalced") Carmelite convent (St. Joseph's) in Avila in 1563. There she wrote *The Way of Perfection* to guide her sisters along the way of deeper union with God that she herself had found.

In 1567, her "public mission" of renewal began when the prior general of the Carmelite order urged Teresa to establish other houses of Carmelites following her stricter observance, a mission that continued until her death in 1582. She found a kindred soul in another Carmelite, St. John of the

Cross,* who was also a great mystic and labored for the reform of the Carmelites among the men, as Teresa had instructed him.

Teresa was remarkable in that her active apostolate did not prevent her from growing ever deeper in union with God, so much so that in 1572 she experienced the fullest possible union with Christ, which she describes as a "spiritual espousal" or "mystical marriage." Nonetheless, to the end Teresa's writings are full of practical wisdom and humor, even with her constant physical suffering. (She is said to have complained to the Lord after a mishap in her travels: "If this is how you treat your friends, it's no wonder you have so few of them!")

By the end of her life Teresa had founded many Carmelite houses and composed numerous spiritual classics, such as *The Interior Castle*. She was canonized in 1622 by Pope Gregory XV. (Feast, October 5.)

Teresa of Calcutta, Mother (1910–99)

Agnes Gonxha Bojaxhiu left her Balkan home at age seventeen to join the Irish Loretto sisters, who sent her to teach in a school for wealthy girls in Calcutta, India. After some years of teaching, Teresa received permission to work among the poor and the sick. She especially reached out to the "poorest of the poor" and helped the terminally ill to die with dignity.

As other young women sought to join Teresa, she founded the Missionaries of Charity in 1950, with the sari as their habit. She became an Indian citizen in that year and later received India's highest humanitarian award for her charitable work. Her order expanded its ministry to include lepers and extended its outreach to many parts of the world.

Intense prayer and Eucharistic adoration for each sister provide the spiritual power for this apostolate. Teresa was also an outspoken advocate of the right to life and said that the greatest poverty in the world was among the people of wealthy nations who aborted their children and killed their elderly and unwanted.

In 1979 Teresa was awarded the Nobel Peace Prize. Often called a "living saint," the cause for her formal canonization began soon after her death in 1999. "Faithfulness, not success" was one of her well-known mottoes.

Tertullian (c.160–c. 225)

Born a Roman centurion's son in Carthage, North Africa, Tertullian received an excellent classical education and became a successful lawyer, practicing in Rome. After converting to Christianity between 193 and 195, he returned to Carthage and became an effective and tireless Catholic apologist. Many of his sayings have become famous: "The blood of martyrs is [the] seed [of the Church]"; "Prayer is the one thing that can conquer God."

In refuting the heretical "Monarchian" teachings of Praxeas, Tertullian explained that God is a single "substance," but with three distinct "Persons" who form a "trinity"—a formula he coined in speaking of God. Though a brilliant man, Tertullian viewed philosophy as a trick used by demons to introduce heresy. In his opinion, faith and reason were distinct and incompatible.

Salvation, said Tertullian, is attained by faith in a crucified Christ—an absurdity to reason. Regarding the relationship between philosophy and revelation, he commented simply, "What has Athens to do with Jerusalem? What concord is there between the Academy and the Church?" Tertullian's view stands in stark contrast with that of St. Justin Martyr,* who saw Christian faith as "true philosophy"—the fulfillment of the philosophers' quest for truth and wisdom.

Like many North Africans, Tertullian sought to be radical in the practice of his faith. Beginning around 203 he was attracted by the challenging prophecies and rigorous asceticism of the Montanist* movement. He finally left the Catholic Church in 213 and remained a Montanist to the end of his life.

In his Montanist writings, Tertullian excoriated Christians who served in the military (soldiers worship idols), widows who remarried (this was adultery), sinful and worldly priests (whose ministry he saw as invalid), and all who engaged in worldly amusements. Nonetheless, the wisdom and power of the writings of his Catholic period, and other works not tainted with Montanism, have earned him lasting respect. Many excerpts from his writings appear in the *Liturgy of the Hours,* and he is known as the "Father of Ecclesiastical Latin" because of his elegant expression in that language.

Theodore of Mopsuestia (c. 350–428)

Theodore and his friend St. John Chrysostom* studied together and were formed in the "Antiochene" school of Christology by the abbot Diodore* (later bishop of Tarsus). Chrysostom urged Theodore to pursue monastic life, which he did. Theodore was ordained a priest in 383 and became bishop of Mopsuestia in

Cilicia in 392, where he served until his death in 428. He supported the anti-Arian teaching of the First Council of Constantinople* of 381 and rejected the Apollinarian* heresies.

Theodore expressed his Christological belief that the Word of God dwelt in an assumed Man (the subject of Christ's human activity) "by good pleasure [that is, by grace] as in a Son." Thus he distinguishes the two natures in Christ, while still seeking to preserve the uniqueness of the way the Word dwells in Jesus. However, St. Cyril of Alexandria* thought that Theodore's expressions divided Christ into two subjects, and thus led the way to the heresy of Nestorius.*

Even though Theodore did not draw the same conclusions as Nestorius, nonetheless, propositions allegedly from Theodore were condemned by the Second Council of Constantinople* in 553. The controversy continues even today over whether Theodore actually was guilty of any false teaching.

Theodosius I (347–95)

Theodosius I was the Catholic Roman emperor who made Christianity the "official" religion of the empire, forbidding public worship of the Roman and Greek gods and closing their temples in 391. He called the First Council of Constantinople* in 381, which reaffirmed the condemnation of Arianism,* and sought to act as a patron of the Church. Though he wielded great power, Theodosius submitted to performing public penance when St. Ambrose* of Milan demanded his repentance for ordering the massacre of seven thousand people in Thessalonica. Thus, Theodosius began a "new breed" of monarch in Europe: the Christian ruler who seeks to promote and guide the growth of the Church, but who is also submitted to the Church's authority.

Thérèse of Lisieux, St. (1873–97)

How did this rather ordinary French girl, who lived as a cloistered Carmelite nun for nine years before dying of tuberculosis at age twenty-four, become one of the most beloved modern Catholic saints, the copatroness of France and of the missions, and a Doctor of the Church? Put simply, St. Thérèse of the Child Jesus taught and lived what she called the "little way" of love: doing everything, even the most mundane, out of fervent love of God.

This spirituality is possible for everyone. It came to light when her religious superior (and blood sister) directed Thérèse in her last years to write her autobiography. *The Story of a Soul* captured the attention and the hearts of millions of Catholics.

Thérèse, who fervently desired to be a missionary, submitted to God's call to the contemplative life, but prayed with all her heart for the conversion of the world. In discerning her vocation in the Church, she found the answer in 1 Corinthians 13, exclaiming: "In the heart of the Church, my mother, I will be love." As she approached her early death, she said that she looked forward to spending her heaven doing good on earth.

For those reasons, Pope John Paul II* declared "The Little Flower" a Doctor of the Church in 1997 and confirmed her "little way" as a universal path to holiness. So many miracles were attributed to her intercession after her death that the Holy See waived the fifty-year delay before canonization required by canon law. She was declared a saint in 1925 by Pope Pius XI,* twenty-eight years after her death. (Feast, October 1.)

Thomas á Kempis (c. 1380–1471)

More properly known as Thomas von Kempen (after his birthplace near Cologne, Germany), this beloved spiritual writer studied under Florentius Radewyns* in a school of the powerful lay renewal movement called the Brethren of the Common Life.* At Radewyns' recommendation he entered a monastery at Agrientenberg, where he was ordained in 1413. There Kempis spent the rest of his life as a "canon regular" writing, preaching, giving spiritual advice, and copying manuscripts. He would have died in anonymity were it not for his chief work, *The Imitation of Christ,* first circulated in 1418. This practical handbook, which instructs and urges toward perfect following of Christ, has become the most widely read Christian book next to the Bible.

Thomas of Celano (1190–1260)

Thomas was the earliest biographer of St. Francis of Assisi,* commissioned by Pope Gregory IX* to write the first biography in 1228, and the second by the minister general of his order in 1246–47. He also wrote the *Legend of St. Clare* and possibly the *Dies Irae.*

Trent, Council of (1545–63)

This great ecumenical council, the nineteenth in the Catholic Church's history, accomplished both a thoroughgoing reform of the Church and a necessary clarification of Catholic doctrine in response to the Protestant Reformation. After many false starts due to political obstacles, the great reform council finally convened at Trent in December 1545 at the behest of Pope Paul III.* Even then, only thirty-four prelates were present at the opening session, but the number grew steadily as the council's work proceeded.

In the first period (1545–47), the council affirmed, in response to Protestant challenges, that God reveals himself through both Sacred Tradition and Sacred Scripture; that Scripture is to be interpreted solely by the Church; that the Vulgate is the authorized Bible; that justification is by faith, but that merit has a role, too; that Jesus instituted seven sacraments; and so on. Disciplinary reforms were also begun.

The second period of Trent (1551–52) further clarified Catholic teaching on the sacraments and reaffirmed the Catholic understanding of the Eucharist as a transubstantiation of the bread and wine into the true Body and Blood of Christ. A revolt of the German princes against Emperor Charles V led to a suspension of the council, which was not resumed until after the pontificate of Paul IV (Caraffa).

The third and final period of Trent (1562–63) was ably led by St. Charles Borromeo.* It completed the clarification of doctrinal issues such as purgatory, indulgences, and the full presence of Christ in either species of the Eucharist. It also established the seminary system, which insured that a well-educated and pure-hearted priesthood would be formed to preach the gospel, administer the sacraments properly, and carry out the reforms that the council had promulgated. The impact of Trent was felt immediately, and its shaping of the life and teaching of the Catholic Church, called "Tridentine Catholicism," continued to be a dominant influence up until the Second Vatican Council* in the 1960s, four hundred years later.

Trullo, Council of (692)

Byzantine emperor Justinian II invited the Eastern bishops to meet in the domed room ("Trullus") of his palace to pass disciplinary decrees, completing the work of the fifth (553) and sixth (680–81) ecumenical councils. However, Pope St. Sergius rejected some of these decrees, such as one declaring that the see of Constantinople is equal to Rome. Although some of the canons of this council were later approved by Pope John VIII for observance in the East, this event illustrates the growing tension and differences at that time between the Church in the East and in the West.

U

Urban II, Blessed Pope (c. 1042–99)

Urban II was a Church reformer and diplomat who continued the "Gregorian Reform" of his predecessor, Pope St. Gregory VII.* He had lived as a monk at Cluny* and served as its prior before being called by Gregory VII to serve as cardinal bishop of Ostia (1080) and as papal legate in Germany. The first years of Urban's papacy, which began in 1088, were focused on reform of the Church and establishing or extending the influence of the papacy and the Church in Europe.

Although exiled for a time through the connivance of Emperor Henry IV, by 1095 Urban's position was strong, and he called two important councils at Piacenza and Clermont. At Clermont, he called for a weekly truce in warfare (the "Truce of God").

He also responded to the plea from Byzantine emperor Alexius I Comnenus for military help to defend the Church in the East from the Muslims. With the cry *"Deus Vult!"* ("God wills it!"), Urban summoned Christian rulers to launch a crusade* to aid Eastern Christians and to deliver Jerusalem from Muslim control.

Urban hoped that this assistance of the Byzantine empire would eventually lead to a healing of the schism between the Church of the East and the West, but it was not to be.

Among his many accomplishments, Urban was the first to use the term "Roman Curia" (*curia Romana*) to describe the offices of papal administration. He also strengthened the College of Cardinals and reorganized papal finances. Urban was beatified in 1881 by Pope Leo XIII.*

Urban VI, Pope (1318–89)

Was this pope elected freely? Did he become mentally unbalanced or deranged after his election? These were the questions surrounding Urban VI, whose election led to the Great Schism* within the Church in the Latin West from 1378–1417.

The situation was this: Gregory XI* had just moved the papacy back to Rome from Avignon after sixty-eight years. When he died only months after his return, the Roman people feared that the next pope would again be French and would move back to Avignon. So the outcry in the streets was for the conclave to elect a Roman, or at least an Italian.

Wisely, the cardinals did elect a sixty-year-old Italian cardinal with a background in canon law and twenty years' experience in the curia at Avignon, who took the title Urban VI. But to the surprise of all and the dismay of many, the new pope directed tirades against the worldliness of cardinals, bishops, kings, queens, and nobility. When some cardinals threatened to return to Avignon on account of this "abuse," the pope said he would simply create enough Italian cardinals to outvote them.

Finally, a number of cardinals (almost all French) met secretly and declared that Urban's election was invalid because they had chosen him under duress. They declared Urban VI deposed and proceeded to elect a new pope (anti-pope)—a Frenchman, Cardinal Robert of Geneva, as "Pope" Clement VII. Thus the Great Schism* began.

The two claimants gathered their armies, and Urban's drove Clement's out of Italy to Avignon. Urban selected an international body of twenty-nine new cardinals and proceeded to govern the Church, ignoring all suggestions and creative schemes to end the schism.

Whether or not Urban VI was actually suffering from a mental illness no one will ever know, though these events raise the question of how the Church should deal with the case of a pope who is mentally unfit to continue in office but refuses to step down. Pope Urban lost the support of many of his cardinals and people and left the papal states in anarchy and the papal treasury empty when he died suddenly (some say of poisoning) in Rome in 1389. But more than half of the Western church, including St. Catherine of Siena,* still considered him to be the true pope.

V

van Ruysbroeck, John (1293–1381)
A Flemish mystical writer, van Ruysbroeck studied in Brussels, living with his uncle John Hinckaert, a holy canon. After he was ordained around 1317, he continued doing pastoral work with his uncle and refuted heresies, especially those of the movement called Brethren of the Free Spirit. He and his uncle, seeking a more solitary life, went to a hermitage in Groenendael near Brussels, which eventually evolved into a community of canons led by van Ruysbroeck.

He began to write a number of mystical works, such as the *Spiritual Espousals*, which became important in the new spiritual and mystical renewal of the time called the *Devotio Moderna*. This spiritual renewal stressed development of a relationship with God through prayer and action, rather than by logic or scholastic philosophy and theology. Sources for his approach were St. Augustine,* St. Bernard of Clairvaux,* St. Bede,* Dionysius the Pseudo-Areopagite,* and Meister Eckhart.* Van Ruysbroeck's hermitage was associated with Catholic renewal movements of the time: the Brethren of the Common Life* and the Canons Regular of Windesheim.

Vatican Council, Second (1962–65)
The twenty-first ecumenical council of the Catholic Church, this council of renewal was called for by Blessed Pope John XXIII* and convened by him in 1962. It was continued by his successor Pope Paul VI,* with a total of four sessions, from 1962 to 1965. The teaching of the Second Vatican Council is contained in sixteen documents, including four constitutions, and is incorporated fully into the *Catechism of the Catholic Church* promulgated by Pope John Paul II* in 1992 and the Code of Canon Law, revised in 1983 according to the Second Vatican Council's teaching. This council ushered in a new era in Catholic life, characterized by more openness to active involvement in the world, worship of God in participatory vernacular language, and a more biblical and patristic expression of doctrine.

Veuillot, Louis (1813–83)
Veuillot was the most outspoken nineteenth-century French proponent of the papacy and opponent of Gallicanism and Liberalism. A lay Catholic, his chief instrument to promulgate his opinions was his newspaper, *L'Univers*. His views were so

hostile to government policies (for example, placing French schools under interfaith supervision), that Veuillot was imprisoned in 1844 and later his paper was suspended (1860–67).

Veuillot fought any attempts to reconcile Church teaching with modern ideas and supported a strong statement of papal infallibility. Pope Pius IX* valued Veuillot's advice, and *L'Univers* became widely read because of the pope's favor. After Veuillot's death in 1883, his brother took over the paper and softened its tone to reflect the more conciliatory policies and approach of Pope Leo XIII.*

Vianney, St. Jean-Baptiste Marie (1786–1859)

The "Curé of Ars," as Vianney is called, is the patron of parish priests because of his holiness and renown as a confessor and preacher. Born near Lyons, France, he studied for the priesthood, but his inability to learn Latin almost disqualified him. Fortunately, his bishop recognized his pastoral gifts and ordained him anyway in 1815.

Vianney was sent to a small village, Ars-en-Dombes, where his powerful preaching and gift of knowledge in the confessional brought masses of people flocking to Ars. Eventually, he spent up to eighteen hours a day hearing confessions. Though he sought many times to be transferred to the peace of a monastery, he remained in Ars, where he died while hearing confessions in 1859. Vianney's purity enabled him to turn away temptations and even physical assaults by the devil. He was canonized by Pope Pius XI* in 1925. (Feast, August 4.)

Vincent of Lèrins, St. (d. before 450)

Though little is known of this monk's life, his writings from the early to mid-fifth century shed light on the Catholic understanding of Christianity. His most famous passage is taken from chapter two of his *Commonitorium*, in which he described the true Catholic faith as "what has been believed everywhere, always, and by all." He insisted that the safeguards against heretical teaching are threefold: the Scripture, the Church as authoritative interpreter of Scripture, and the ecumenical council.

Vitalian, Pope St. (d. 672)

Vitalian (pope 637–72) is known for his support of the Church's growth in England in allegiance to Rome. He is also remembered for his stand against the Monothelite heresy, which held that Jesus had only one will—the divine will. He wrote in opposition to this heresy after the death of the Byzantine emperor Constans II, who had supported it. In addition, Vitalian helped implement the decisions of the Synod of Whitby* (664) that ruled in favor of the celebration of Easter in Britain according to the Roman calendar.

Vladimir, St. (956–1015)

It was a remarkable event when Prince Vladimir's grandmother, Olga, was baptized in Constantinople. It was a world-shaking event when the powerful young prince himself decided (perhaps for interests of state) to embrace Eastern Orthodox Christianity for himself and his people in 988. The religion of the Rus tribe—the Russian people—was determined by that decision, which unified them in the Christian (Orthodox) faith and brought his kingdom, based in Kiev, into a positive political relationship with the Byzantine Empire.

Vladimir favored the Church in law; for example, he granted clergy immunity from civil law and encouraged people to tithe. He also actively practiced the Christian faith himself: He established monasteries, constructed churches, cared for the hungry, gave money and food to the poor, and opposed capital punishment.

Voltaire (1694–1778)

François Marie Arouet, writing under the pseudonym "Voltaire," was France's leading eighteenth-century critic of the Catholic Church. His biting satires, directed against both Church and crown, led to a three-year exile in England (1726–29). While in England, he praised the rational deism of John Locke and attacked the "fanatic" Christianity of George Fox (founder of the Quakers) and of his countryman of the previous century, Blaise Pascal.*

Later, in his best-known work, *Candide* (1759), Voltaire mocked the optimism of German philosopher Gottfried Leibniz and his claim that this world is "the best of all possible worlds." Voltaire was a convinced deist who believed in a god who is the author of moral values, which all people are bound to observe. He advocated religious toleration and the practice of virtue, which appealed to many who rejected religious dogmatism and intolerance.

von Balthasar, Hans Urs (1905–88)

Von Balthasar was a Swiss theologian whose diverse writings attracted much attention in the late twentieth century. He joined the Society of Jesus shortly after earning his doctorate in philosophy in 1928. He was ordained in 1936 and served as a spiritual director to students in Basel, including noted convert-mystic Adrienne von Speyr.

In 1950 he left the Jesuits and founded the "Community of St. John" in Basel. He also founded the international theological journal *Communio* and authored an ambitious three-part work, *The Glory of the Lord: A Theological Aesthetics.* For his contributions to Catholic theology he was named a cardinal by Pope John Paul II* shortly before his death in 1988.

von Hügel, Friedrich (1852–1925)

A leading Catholic lay intellectual, von Hügel was a distinguished continental spiritual counselor and expert in spirituality and the philosophy of religion. He is associated with the "modernist" movement through his friendship with Alfred Loisy* and George Tyrrell, but he remained within the Catholic Church. He was a mystic emphasizing the transcendence of God and the centrality of adoration, though he also advised Evelyn Underhill, the expert on mysticism, to spend two afternoons a week visiting the poor. Among his books was *The Mystical Element of Religion As Studied in St. Catherine of Genoa and Her Friends* (1908).

Waldenses (or Waldensians/Vaudois)
This movement was named after Peter Valdes (Waldo), a wealthy citizen of Lyons, who (around 1170) experienced a conversion, gave away his wealth, and began preaching among the poor. His way of life was approved at the Third Lateran Council* (1179), stipulating that his followers could only preach when authorized by the local clergy. However, because many clergy were lax, worldly, and didn't preach at all, the Waldensians often preached without permission. They were excommunicated in 1182 or 1183.

These "Poor Men of Lyons" continued to preach and serve the poor and became more critical of the Catholic understanding of the priesthood, the sacraments, and some points of doctrine (such as purgatory). Although the Waldenses hated the dualistic theology of the Albigensians,* they were persecuted along with them. Many of those who remained unreconciled with the Catholic Church later joined other groups that broke away, such as the Hussites* in Bohemia in the fifteenth century and the various streams of sixteenth-century Protestantism.

Some Waldenses, however, were reconciled with the Catholic Church, especially through the work of Pope Innocent III* in the early thirteenth century. These groups were called the "Poor Catholics" in Spain, led by Duran of Huesca, and in Italy the "Poor (or Reconciled) Lombards" under Bernard Prim. Neither group grew very large, and they were overshadowed by the followers of St. Francis* and St. Dominic.*

Wenceslas, St. (c. 907–c. 929)
This patron saint of Bohemia was raised a Catholic, particularly through the influence of his grandmother, St. Ludmilla. Wenceslas' unstable mother, Drahomira, had Ludmilla murdered and ruled as regent upon the death of her husband, the Duke of Wratislaw. Urged by the people, Wenceslas wrested control of the government from his mother in 922 and proved himself to be a pious and enlightened ruler, promoting religion, culture, and peaceful relationships with Western states (especially Germany).

When his jealous brother Boleslav murdered him (c. 929 or 935), Wencelas was immediately honored as a martyr. His relics were brought to St. Vitus church in Prague, which became a major pilgrimage site. (Feast, September 28.)

Westphalia, Peace of (1648)

The Peace of Westphalia comprised two treaties that ended the Thirty Years' War (1618–48), which was primarily a conflict between Catholic and Protestant forces in Central Europe. The Holy Roman Empire, now in severe decline, negotiated treaties with France at Münster (in Westphalia) and with Sweden and other Protestant states at Osnabrück. Among other things, these treaties recognized the Calvinists as having the right to political control of a territory and called for the "secularization" (takeover) of much Church property by the states as compensation for war expenses.

Pope Innocent X vainly protested both the takeover of Church lands and the political recognition of Calvinist states. On the positive side, the peace did succeed substantially in ending the bloodshed.

Whitby, Synod of (664)

After growing tension between the Roman and Celtic (Irish) missionaries in England, King Oswin called together representatives from both sides to judge between them. St. Bede* recounts the meeting in his *History of the English Church and People*. King Oswin decided that because St. Peter had greater authority than the saints of the Irish tradition, the Catholic Church in England would follow the practices of Rome (founded by St. Peter) and maintain allegiance to the pope.

St. Cuthbert, representing the Celtic tradition, agreed to adapt to the Roman rite. A priest of the Lindisfarne monastery, Cuthbert later served as bishop of Hexham and finally bishop of Lindisfarne before his death in 687.

Wilfrid, St. (634–709)

Wilfrid was a leading voice at the Synod of Whitby* (644) for the Church in England to observe Easter according to the Roman calendar. He began his career as a monk at the Celtic monastery of Lindisfarne and then studied in Canterbury, Rome, and Lyons. He became firmly convinced that the Church in England should follow the observances of the see of St. Peter and the monastic tradition of St. Benedict.* Wilfrid implemented this policy as bishop of York, but he also suffered persecution because of his allegiance to Rome.

Providentially, these conflicts enabled him to do missionary work. He ended up preaching in Frisia (modern Holland) on his way to Rome to make an appeal to the pope. Later he ministered to the heathen in northern England when a dispute with the archbishop of Canterbury forced him to abandon his see from 681–86. Wilfrid spread the faith to new lands, helped draw the Church in England into a closer allegiance to Rome, and promoted the monastic life following St. Benedict's rule. (Feast, October 12.)

William of Ockham (c. 1285–1347)
Ockham (also Occam) was a controversial and creative English thinker of the fourteenth century. He joined the Franciscan order and studied and taught at Oxford, until he was accused of teaching false doctrine by the chancellor of the university. Fifty-one propositions in Ockham's writings were censured by Pope John XXII.

A few years later Ockham accused the pope of holding heretical positions in his condemnation of radical Franciscan poverty. Finally, Ockham was excommunicated in 1328 and expelled from the Franciscan order in 1331. In 1328 he fled to the court of Emperor Louis the Bavarian, where he spent the rest of his days writing and attacking papal authority in the temporal sphere.

As a logician, Ockham's intellectual legacy is rich. His famous philosophical principle known as "Ockham's razor" attacks unnecessary multiplication of causes, and he denied the existence of universals. He refuted any proofs of God's existence or qualities, relying on revelation for any sure knowledge of God. Hence, Ockham gave rise to the *via moderna* of nominalism, which denies the positive relationship of reason and faith. He also limited the pope's authority to the spiritual realm, though he claimed that an emperor could and should depose a heretical pope.

In summary, William paved the way for a new era in Christian thought and Church-state relations. His attack on scholasticism became widely known in the universities; his teaching on the limitations of papal authority gave rise to conciliar theory, and his nominalist philosophy influenced Gabriel Biel,* who taught Martin Luther,* emphasizing the separation of faith and reason.

William of Rubruck (d. after 1256)
William was a Franciscan missionary sent by King St. Louis IX* in 1253 to find and evangelize the Mongol khan. He found Batu Khan, who sent him on to the Great Khan north of the Caspian Sea. William remained in that khan's court for two years and returned, writing an account of the journey for King Louis.

Worms, Concordat of (1122)

This landmark agreement between Pope Callistus II and German emperor Henry V ended the worst abuses of lay investiture. Henceforth, secular rulers could invest bishops and abbots with symbols of temporal power (for example, a scepter), but they could not interfere with the free canonical election and consecration of Church leaders, nor invest them with the symbols of their spiritual authority (ring and crozier). This compromise agreement ended the prolonged bitter dispute between the Church and the empire over investiture. The agreement was confirmed by the First Lateran Council (the ninth ecumenical council), held in Rome in 1123.

Worms, Diet of (1521)

Emperor Charles V summoned Martin Luther* to a series of inquests in 1521 at Worms to explain his teachings. Luther appeared on April 16 and refused to recant his beliefs, saying, "Here I stand. I can do no other. God help me. Amen." Luther left after ten days, taking refuge at Wartburg Castle under the protection of the Elector Frederick of Saxony. On May 25, 1521, the diet issued the Edict of Worms, declaring Luther a heretic.

Wycliffe, John (c. 1330–84)

An English priest, philosopher, and theologian (doctorate from Oxford, 1372), Wycliffe sparked controversy by contesting Catholic doctrines such as transubstantiation (Wycliffe said the Eucharist remains bread), the authority of the Church (one owes obedience only to Christ), indulgences, private confession, and justification by faith and works. In short, Wycliffe anticipated the main tenets of Martin Luther* and the Protestant reformers two centuries later. In his own lifetime, John Huss* and the Czech reformers followed Wycliffe's teaching.

Wycliffe also believed that the Bible should be read in one's own language, so he undertook an English translation, assisted and completed by his friend John Purvey. Though his doctrine was renounced by the Catholic Church and his followers forced to renounce Wycliffite teaching, Wycliffe himself was protected by powerful political figures who wished England to be free from "Roman" church control and taxation. Hence, he died a free man in 1384, although the Council of Constance* (1414–18) condemned his teaching. The followers of Wycliffe in England were called "Lollards."

Xavier, St. Francis (1506–52)

One of the original members of the Society of Jesus (Jesuits), this aristocratic Spaniard met Ignatius of Loyola* while studying at the University of Paris. Though initially unimpressed by Ignatius, Francis ended up taking vows of poverty and chastity with him in 1534 and in 1537 was ordained a priest with all the first Jesuits in Venice. When the Portuguese asked Pope Paul III* for missionaries to evangelize the East, Francis immediately gave up his position as secretary of the order and sailed from Lisbon to Goa in South India.

Beginning his missionary work in 1542, Francis preached and baptized throughout southern India and Ceylon (Sri Lanka). In 1549 he traveled to Japan and, after learning some Japanese, formed a church that endured great persecution. He returned to Goa in 1552 to prepare to evangelize China (his dream), but he fell ill and died on an island just off the coast of China as he was preparing to enter secretly.

Francis' body was returned to Goa, where it rests today in the Church of the Good Jesus. His arm, which is said to have baptized as many as 700,000 people in his ten years of mission, is enshrined in the Jesuit Church (the "Jesu") in Rome. St. Francis was canonized in 1622 and was declared patron saint of foreign missionaries by Pope (St.) Pius X.* (Feast, December 3.)

Ximénez de Cisneros, Francisco (1436–1517)

A vigorous Church reformer, Ximénez held many prominent positions in the Church in Spain. He entered a Franciscan Observatine community in Toledo in 1481 and adopted a lifestyle of severe asceticism and prayer that he maintained to the end of his life. He became the confessor of Queen Isabella in 1492, and with her support reformed the Franciscan Order and other religious communities.

In 1495, Ximénez reluctantly (at the pope's command) accepted the office of archbishop of Toledo, which carried much secular power. Despite his prominence, he continued to live an ascetic life and used his money to found the University of Alcala in 1500, which became a center of Renaissance learning in Spain. He was made a cardinal in 1507 and continued faithfully to serve his country and the Church until his death in 1517. The Protestant Reformation did not succeed in Spain because the Catholic Church had already been reformed and strengthened before Martin Luther,* due largely to the zeal of leaders such as Ximénez.

Z

Zwingli, Ulrich (1484–1531)

A Swiss Catholic, Zwingli was ordained a priest in 1506 and was pastor in the town of Glarus for ten years. Influenced by Erasmus,* he learned Greek and some Hebrew and began to read the fathers of the Church. However, while a chaplain at the famous Marian shrine at Einsiedeln, he was scandalized by pious excesses and gradually grew critical of the Catholic Church.

Zwingli's break from Rome came around 1518 when he began to preach against the Catholic Church in Zurich, where he had been called to preach. Zurich became a center of Zwingli's "reforms," which included abolishing the Mass, removing all images and paintings from the churches, and instituting a daily session of Bible reading and exegesis. Zwingli rejected both the Catholic view and Martin Luther's* view of the Eucharist, holding instead that the bread and wine merely symbolize the presence of Christ.

While rejecting the Catholic Eucharist, he nevertheless maintained the validity of infant baptism against the Anabaptist* groups that sprang up in Zurich. His response to their growth in that city was to have their leaders drowned. Zwingli died in 1531 in a battle against an army of Catholic cantons. Though he did not found a major church as Luther did, Zwingli's more radical interpretation of the Bible was imitated by Jean Calvin* and later Protestant reformers.